Grafton and Bolton Ontario and Area in Colour Photos, Saving Our History One Photo at a Time

Photography by Barbara Raué
©2019

Series Name: Cruising Ontario

Book 224: Grafton, Bolton and Area

Cover photo: 45 Nancy Street, Page 36

©All the photos in this book have been taken with my cameras. I own the rights to them.

Series Name: Cruising Ontario
Saving Our History One Photo at a Time
in colour photos

Books Available in Alphabetical Order:
Aberfoyle, Acton, Ajax, Alton, Amherstburg, Ancaster, Arthur, Auburn, Aylmer, Ayr, Beaver Valley, Belgrave, Belleville, Bloomingdale, Blyth, Brantford, Brockville, Burford, Burlington, Caledon, Caledonia, Cambridge, Carlow, Chatsworth, Clifford, Collingwood, Conestogo, Delhi, Dorchester to Aylmer, Drayton, Drumbo, Dundas, Dunlop, Eden Mills, Elmira, Elora, Erin, Essex, Fergus, Goderich, Grimsby, Guelph, Hagersville, Hamilton, Hanover, Harriston, Hespeler, Jarvis, Kingston, Kingsville, Kitchener, Lake Superior, Lincoln, Linwood, Listowel, London, Lucknow, Merrickville, Mono, Mount Forest, Mount Pleasant, Neustadt, New Hamburg, Newboro, Newport, Niagara-on-the-Lake, Niagara Falls, North Bay, Oakville, Onondaga, Orangeville, Orillia, Oshawa, Owen Sound, Palmerston, Paris, Pelham, Perth, Peterborough, Petrolia, Pickering, Port Colborne, Port Elgin, Portland, Preston, Rockwood, Sarnia, Sault Ste. Marie, Seaforth, Sheffield, Shelburne, Simcoe, Smiths Falls, Smithville, Southampton, St. Catharines, St. George, St. Jacobs, St. Marys, St. Thomas, Stoney Creek, Stratford, Thamesford, Thunder Bay, Tillsonburg, Toronto, Waterdown, Waterford, Waterloo, Welland, Wellesley, West Flamborough, Westport, Whitby, Windsor, Wingham, Woodstock

Book 216: Sudbury
Book 217: Parry Sound
Book 218-219: Uxbridge
Book 220: Port Perry
Book 221-222: Stouffville
Book 223: Colborne

Book 224: Grafton, Bolton

Table of Contents

Grafton	Page 7
Bolton	Page 29
Sandhill	Page 67
Campbell's Cross	Page 68

    The Township of Alnwick/Haldimand is located in central Ontario in Northumberland County, situated between Lake Ontario and Rice Lake. It was formed in 2001 by the merger of Alnwick Township in the north and Haldimand Township in the south.

    Alnwick Township was originally surveyed in 1795 when twenty-four lots were laid out on the first concession. It was named for Alnwick in Northumberland, England. The township's first residents were made up of United Empire Loyalists, attracted by large unencumbered land grants, sometimes in the thousands of acres. In 1835, 3,600 acres of land along the first and second concessions were set aside as an Indian settlement. Shortly after, the Indian Band from Grape Island was moved into this settlement and a school and church were built at Alderville. The first council meeting was held in 1845 at Alderville School. The Alnwick/Haldimand Township building located in Grafton was built in 1858. Prior to its construction, Township Council meetings were held at local taverns or the residences of council members.

Haldimand Township was formed in 1791 and was named in honor of Sir Frederick Haldimand – a British general who served as Governor-in-Chief of Canada between 1778 and 1796. By 1804, there were 356 settlers in Haldimand Township making it the second most populous township in the region after Hamilton Township to the West. The town hall was constructed in 1860.

As part of provincial initiatives in the late 1990s, the Government of Ontario pursued a policy of municipal amalgamations to reduce waste and duplication. Alnwick Township and Haldimand Township became a single Township of Alnwick/Haldimand on January 1, 2001.

Alnwick/Haldimand is part of the Oak Ridges Moraine. Thirty-one square kilometers of the Cobourg Creek watershed runs through the Township. The Creek supports a diverse ecosystem including forests, meadows and wetlands. Numerous species inhabit the Creek including brown trout, rainbow trout, scuplins and darters. Migratory Chinook Salmon spawn in the creek and Atlantic Salmon are being stocked as part of a provincial initiative to return these native fish to Lake Ontario. The Ganaraska Forest is an 11,000-acre forest located in the Township. It is one of the largest blocks of forested land in southern Ontario. The Millvalley Hills Forest is a 297 hectare forest located within the Township. The dominant trees species are red and white pine, and red and white oak. The township is rural based with agriculture being the largest contributor to the economy. Grain, cash crops, milk, livestock, vineyards and apple farming are all viable in the area. Grafton is located in this township.

The first known settlers to Grafton were just before the turn of the 19th century. These earliest settlers were all from the new United States of America. Most were looking for new land and opportunities, a few were second generation United Empire Loyalists born in loyalist settlements further east.

New settlers from the British Isles started arriving twenty years later. These early Grafton settlers, as well as clearing agricultural land from the forests, produced many fine political leaders. David Rogers was the first to propose anti-slavery legislation for Upper Canada, and Henry Ruttan was the Speaker of the Legislature. Likely the hamlet was named Grafton after John Grover's birth town of Grafton, Massachusetts. He initially arrived in Upper Canada in 1798 and was in Grafton by 1804.

Bolton is a community in the town of Caledon, located in the Region of Peel about fifty kilometres northwest of Toronto. The downtown and area that historically defined the village is in a valley, through which the Humber River flows. The town was founded around 1822 when James Bolton helped build a flour mill for his relative George Bolton. It was established on the line of the Toronto, Grey and Bruce Railway with stages to and from Weston.

In the Humber River valley, George Bolton, newly arrived from England, and his uncle, James, an area pioneer from just after the completion of the 1819 survey, built a grist mill at a bend in the river on land George had purchased from the surveyor, William Chewett. This mill became the catalyst for several other enterprises which became the seed of a hamlet. The village was strongly Reform during the Mackenzie years and James Bolton had to seek refuge in the U.S.A. after the failed rebellion of 1837. In 1842, his son James C. Bolton purchased the mill site from his uncle and built a large flour mill at the site of the current Humberlea Road, as well as a sawmill. The flour mill, in place until 1968, prospered under several prominent mill owners following Bolton including John Guardhouse and Andrew McFall, both of whose homes still survive along King Street East. The village continued to expand driven by water-powered industries such as William Dick's Agricultural Works.

While most evidence of the original mills and other industries have disappeared, the nineteenth century residential fabric remain largely intact and enough survives of the late nineteenth commercial core to maintain the sense of the historic village. As it now stands, the area is characterized by the polychromatic brickwork of the second half of the 19th century in local brick with many of the finer homes incorporating a gabled 'L' plan with a veranda at the inside corner.

Sandhill Ontario is about 9 miles east of Caledon.

Abraham Campbell's father and six brothers took up one thousand acres in Chingacousy about 1820, after having journeyed from the old family home in Lincoln County by an ox-team. From Cooksville to their locations, the way led over a road made through the bush with their own axes. Mr. Campbell spent his life on the farm on which he was born when Chingacousy was the farthest settlement north of the lake. A quarter of a century later Campbell's Cross, on the highway connecting north and south, was a scene of bustling life. There was a tavern there with eighteen rooms. There were three stores in the village at that time. As many as one hundred teams from the North Country would arrive with grain in a single day. Part of the grain was bought by local merchants and teamed by them to Port Credit for shipment by water. Some of the farmers hauled their own grain all the way to the lake port.

Grafton

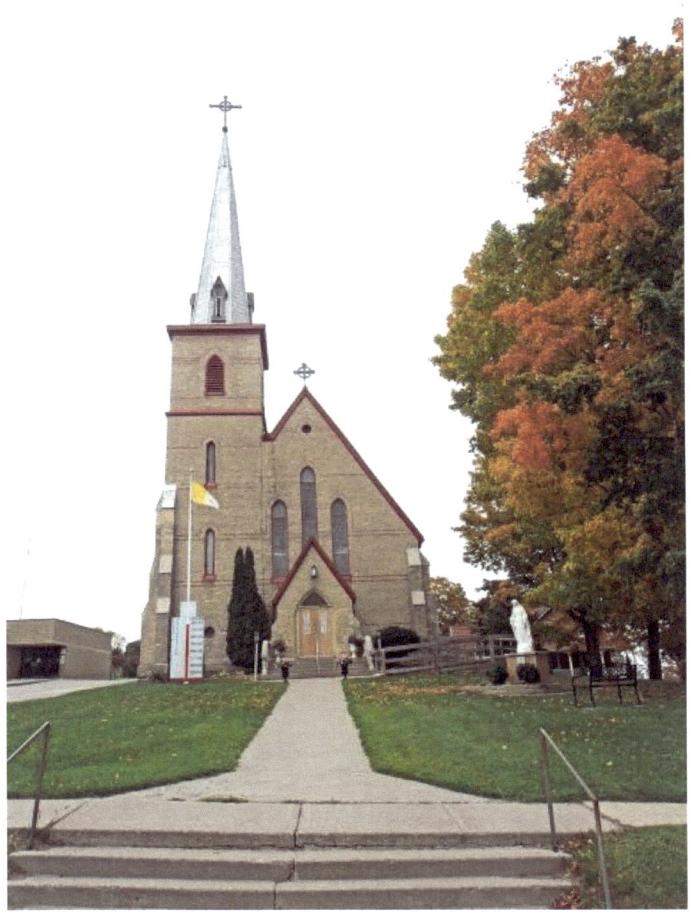

103 Lyle Street South - St. Mary's Roman Catholic Church - The parish dates back to the 1850s when the area served as a mission out of Cobourg. This simple Gothic Revival yellow brick church was built in 1875. In the tradition of rural life and community, it is recorded that the protestant churches of all denominations made significant donations to the building of their neighbor's church. St. Mary's cemetery, behind the church, is the resting place of many of Grafton's early Irish settlers.

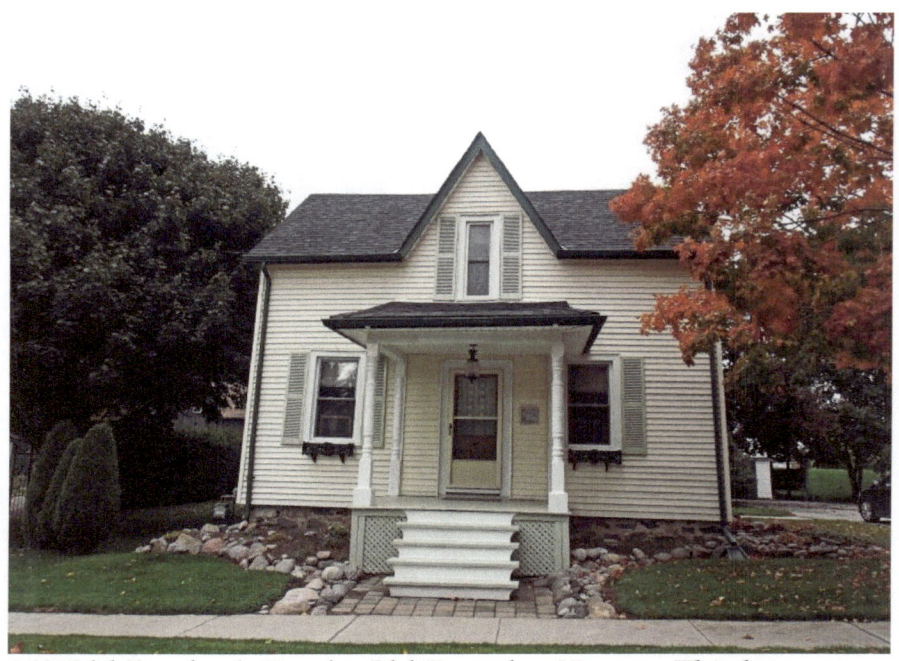

160 Old Danforth Road - Old Foundry House - This house was originally a cabin built around the same time as the barn and was probably for the foundry manager. For a few years it was the rectory for St. Mary's Church before the current rectory, on the hill above the church, was built.

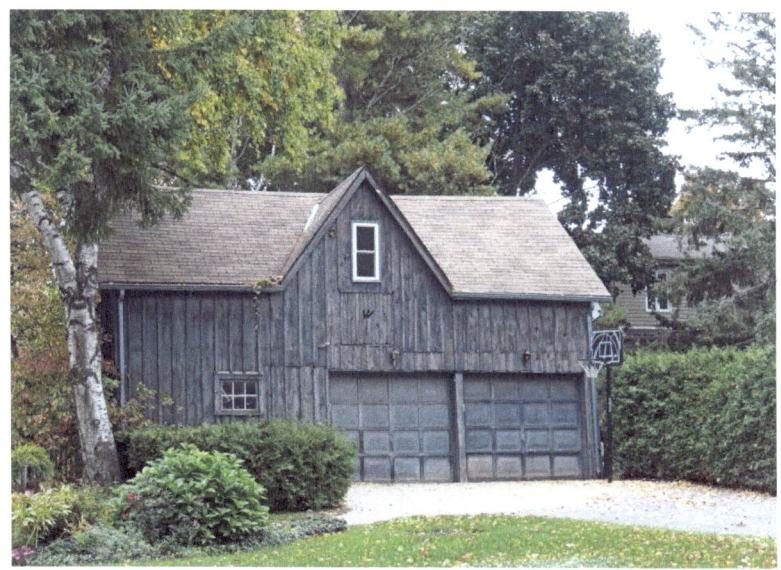

The board and batten barn was built c. 1840 and was a foundry.

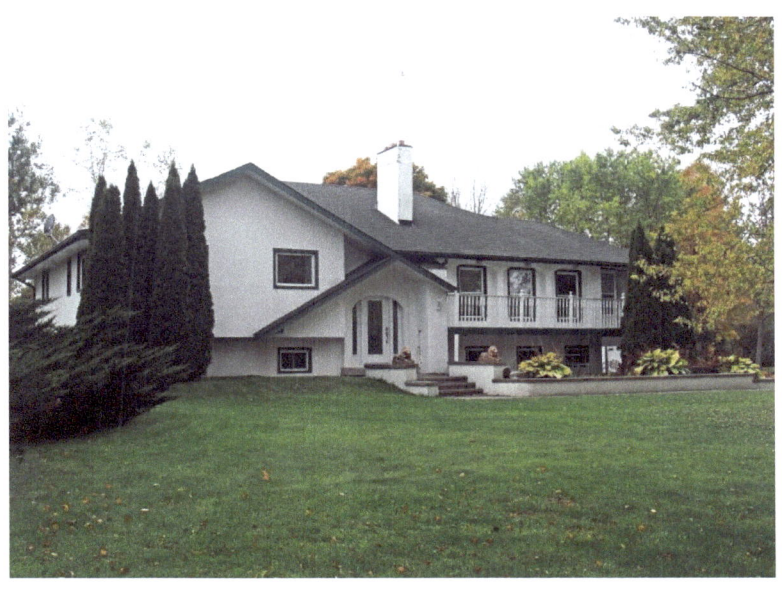

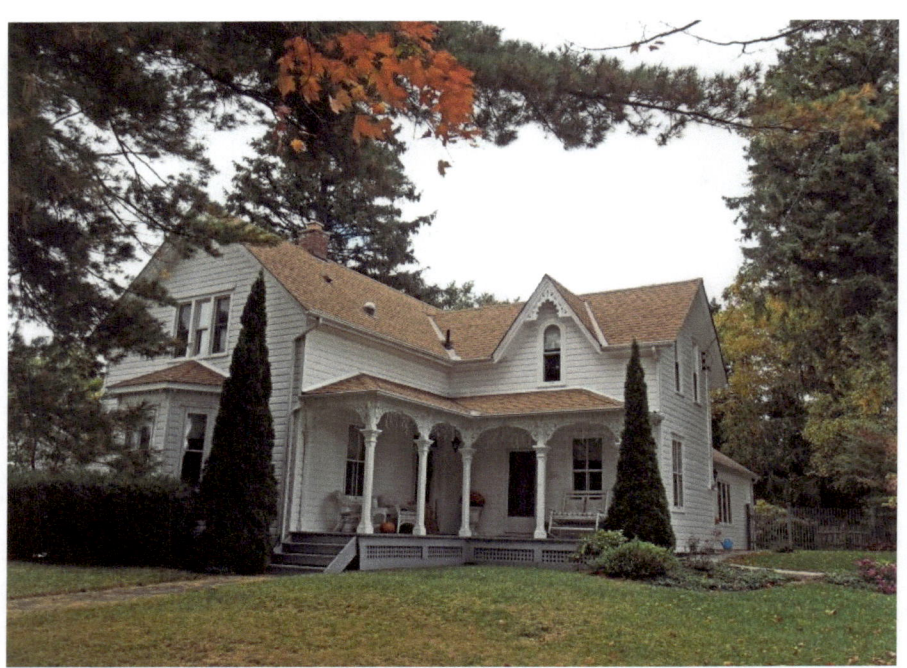

154 Old Danforth Road - The Reuben Lawless House was built in 1870 and is mid-Victorian of the Italianate Vernacular, with "gingerbread". It has a stone/ rubble foundation and cedar siding and is of a balloon structure. The back "extension" was a woodshed/ summer kitchen built over the original well. In 1897 Thomas Lawless became the property owner and in 1900 Reuben Lawless Senior gained title. For years it was known as the Reuben Lawless House and stayed in the Lawless family until 1970.

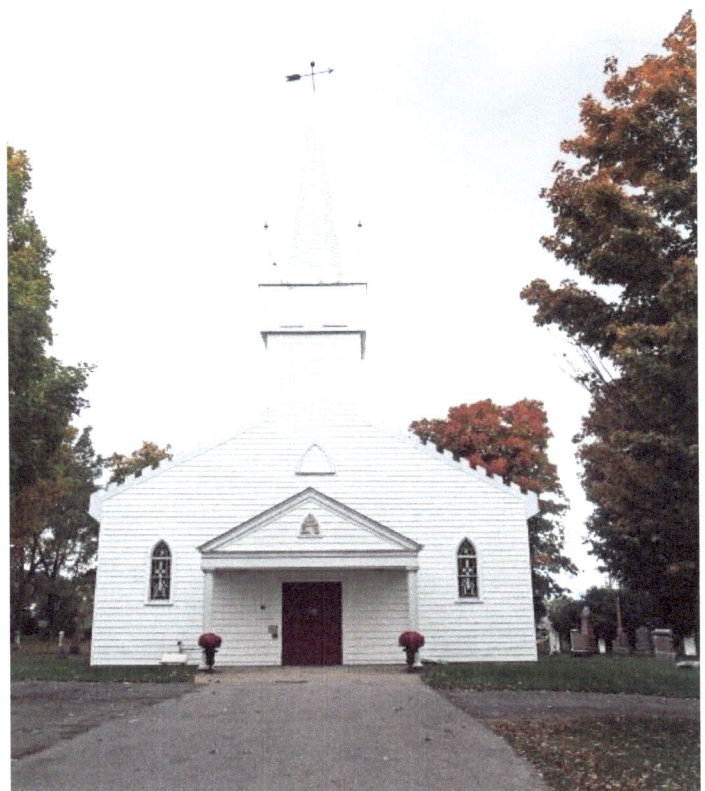

137 Old Danforth Road - St. Andrew's United Church and cemetery - This church, originally Presbyterian, was built in 1844 on land donated by John Grover, an early settler, farmer, innkeeper and storekeeper. One of the requirements that went with the deed of land was that a family plot in the cemetery be reserved for his heirs and also that he have a pew in the church, numbered nine. In spite of the classical profile and symmetrical composition, the crenellations and pointed arches distinguish this early Gothic Revival church. The church is now sided in aluminum and has a new front entrance. To the left of the entrance is a stone memorial to John Grover.

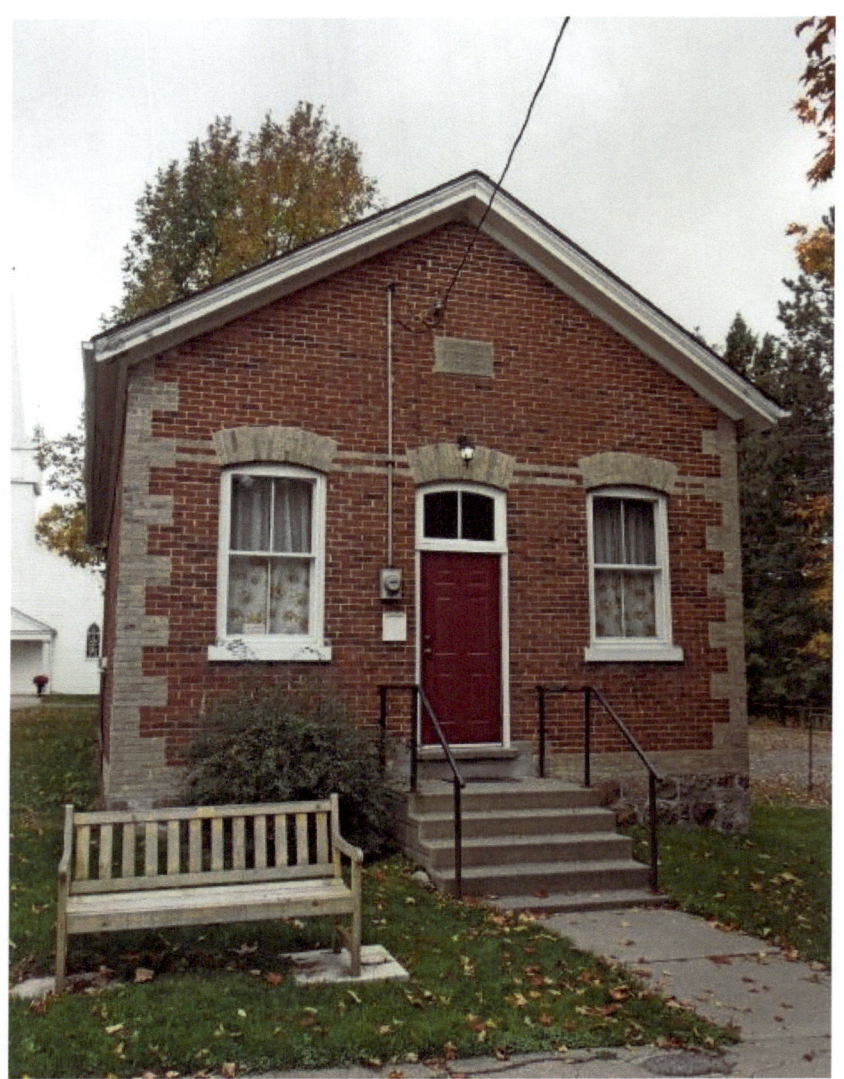

135 Old Danforth Road - Old Presbyterian Sunday School was built in 1884. For many years it served as the Grafton Library. Architecturally it is notable for its patterned dichromatic brick work. There is a strong transom band, quoins and a foundation band topping a squared stone foundation, typically the work of Scottish masons.

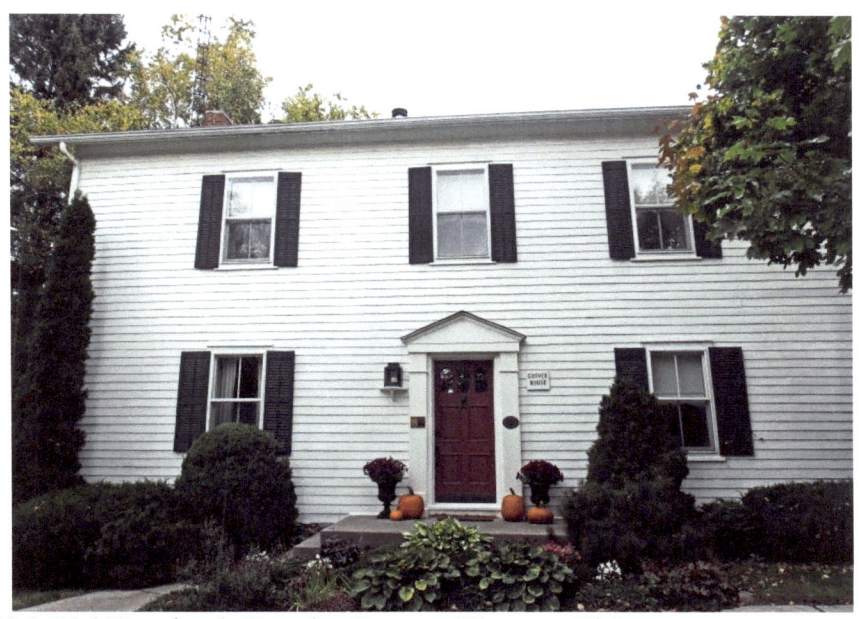

136 Old Danforth Road - Grover House - This two-storey (white with dark green shutters) symmetrical designed house with central front door typifies the Georgian style. It was built in c. 1822 by John Grover, an early (1798) settler from Grafton Massachusetts. The hamlet was named after his home town. The original windows would have had 9 over 9, small glass panes. The replacement windows and white cedar clapboard are probably from around 1900. The clapboard still covers the original cedar shingle siding. John Grover gave the land, across from his house, to the Presbyterian Church, now United Church.

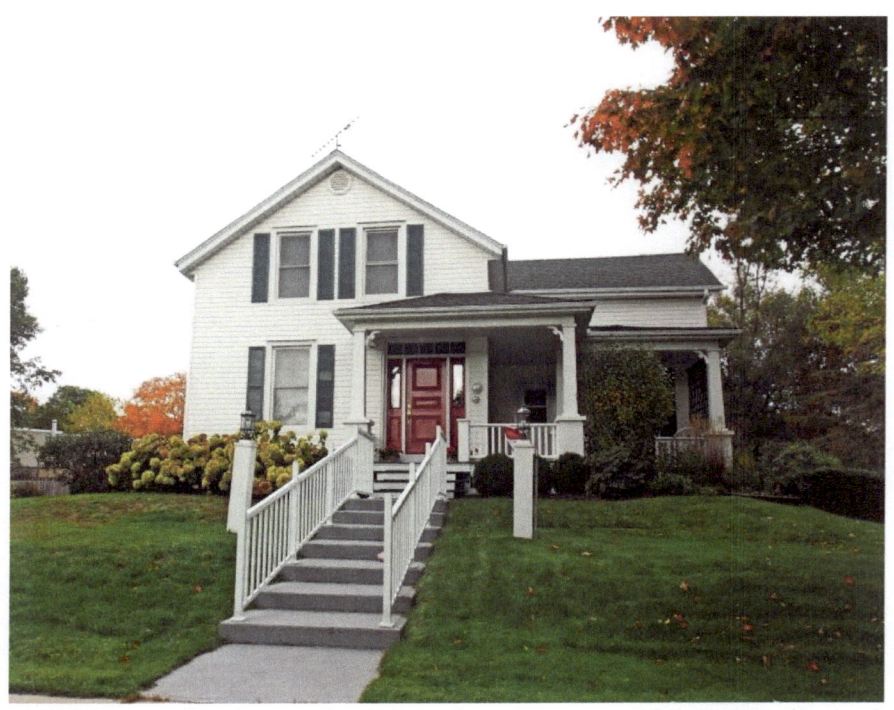

126 Old Danforth Road - A Lawless House - This is the first of the "Lawless" homes. It was built in 1887 by the Lawless family - from old pictures it was very much like the house at 154 with ornate gingerbread trim. These two properties, along with the Grover House were all owned by members of the Lawless family for about 70 years.

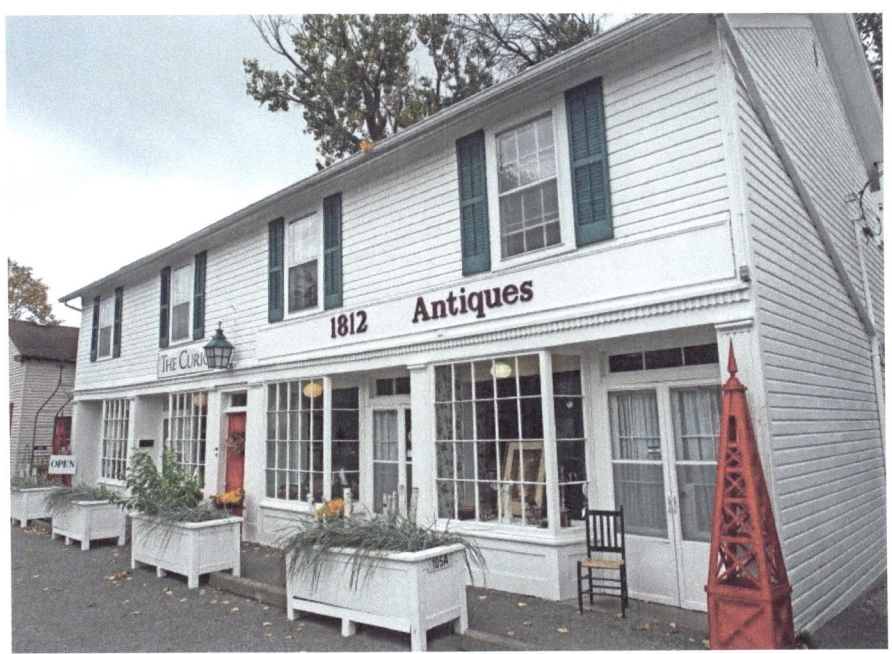

105 Old Danforth Road - 1812 Heritage Building was built in the classic commercial architectural style. This building has housed a barber shop, a post office and a general store at various times. The pleasing façade is of architectural note: its simplicity, finely detailed windows and repetition of elements give it an unusual grace

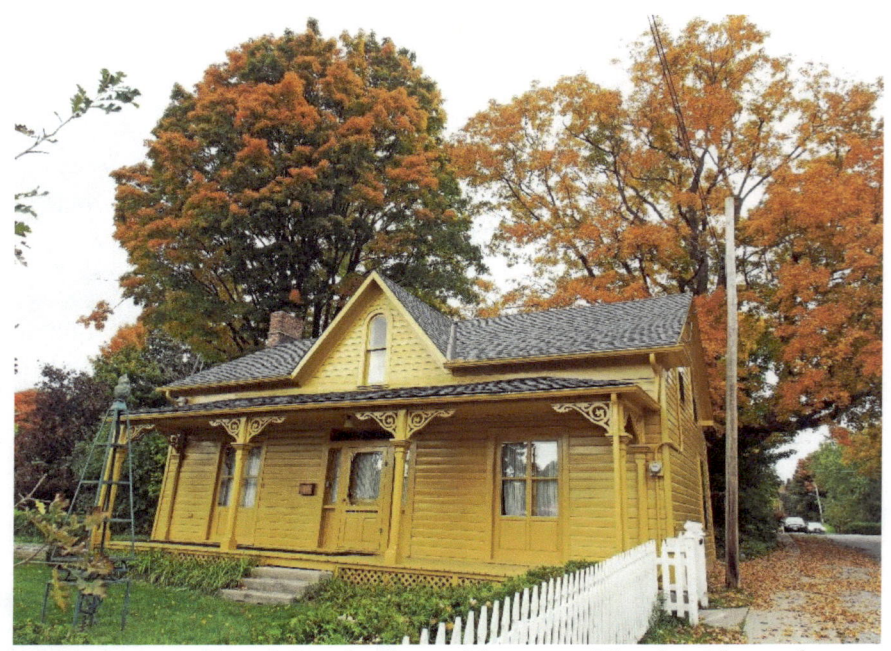

10846 County Road 2 - clapboard house - The façade and gentle slope of the veranda roof of this Gothic Revival style show the influence of Regency architecture. The reproduction picket fence is appropriate to the era and the exterior wood is the original siding. Built in 1859, it consists of balloon framing and has no interior supporting walls (as in barn framing).

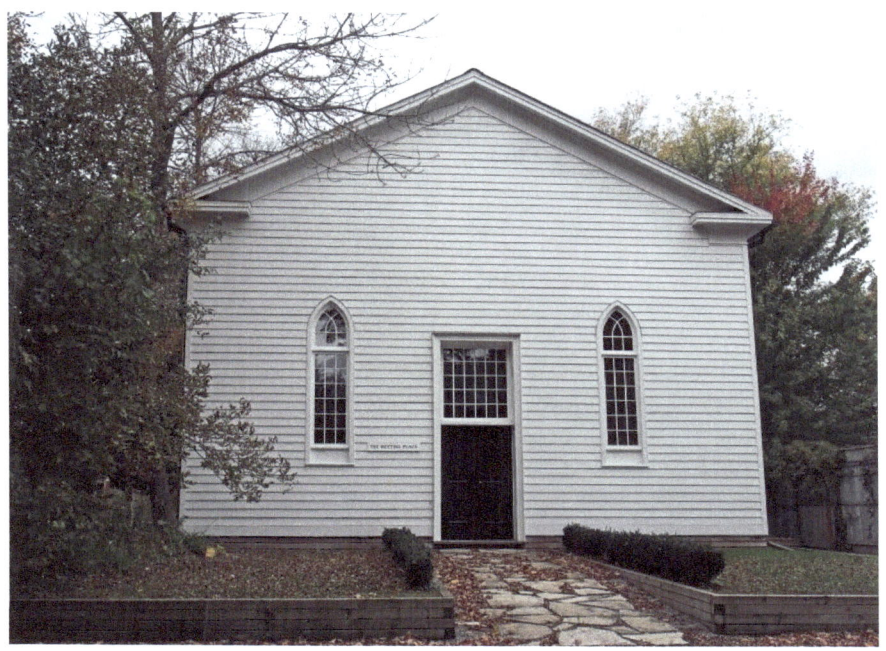

118 Aird Street - Methodist Meeting Hall - In 1856, the Wesleyan Methodist congregation of the township acquired half an acre of land on which the cemetery, Meeting House and house to the north were located. The vernacular timber frame building has certain Neo-Classical elements and strong cornice returns. The last service was held in 1925. Since then, the Hall has been privately owned, but over time had deteriorated and became derelict. A new owner has restored it to its original state.

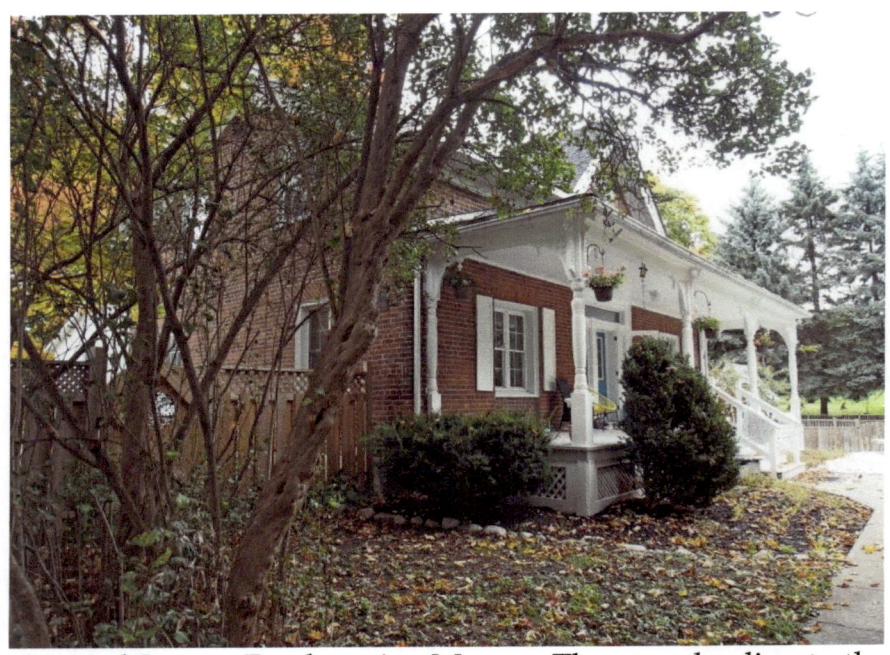

121 Aird Street - Presbyterian Manse - The steps leading to the property retain an early horse-hitching ring. The half-acre on which the house stands was acquired in 1850 and the Gothic Revival home was built prior to 1859. Floor length windows have been altered. Remaining verge board, front door surround and veranda add to the character of this building.

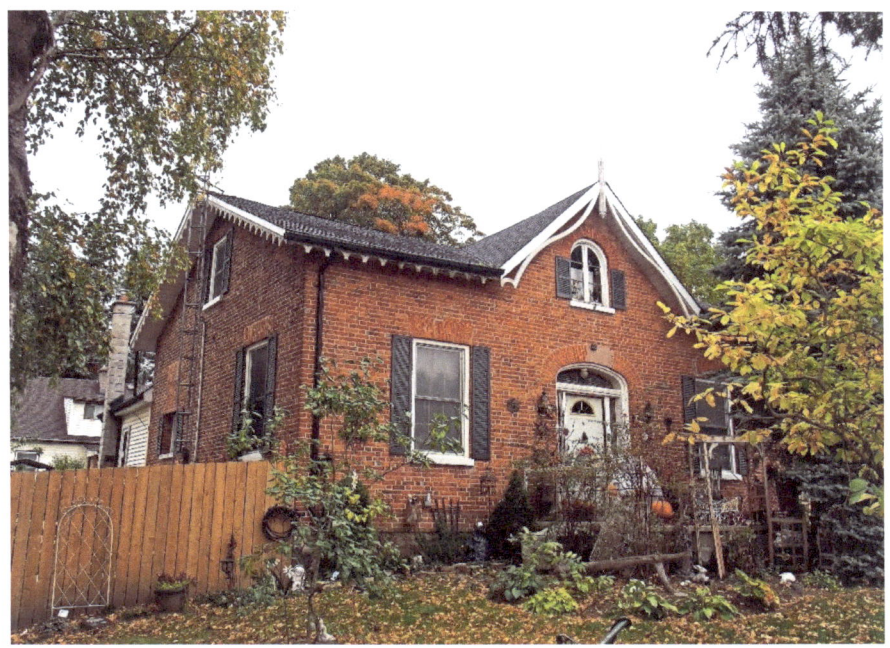

10856 County Road 2 - Patterson House Three doors to the west is the 1861 residence of Eleanor Patterson, the wife of William Patterson, whose family operated inns in Grafton from 1834 to 1890. Restrained verge board, finial and rounded gable entrance enhance the appearance of this home.

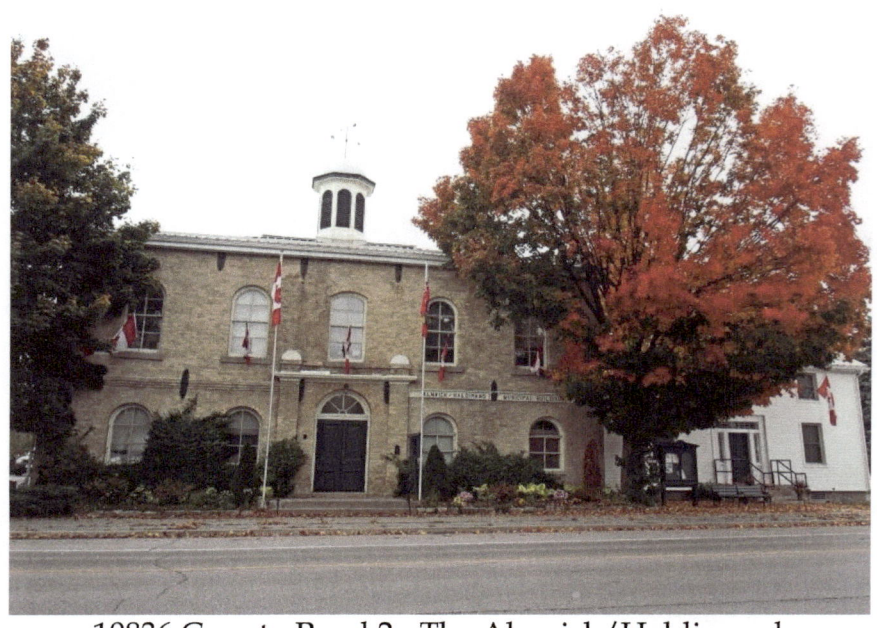

10836 County Road 2 - The Alnwick/Haldimand Township building was built in 1858. Prior to 1858, Township Council meetings were held at local taverns and residences of council members. The lower storey of the building was originally designed to house businesses while the upper floor was used as council chambers and for a variety of social and cultural events. General stores occupied alternate sides of the building in the nineteenth century. In 1907, the Standard Bank took over the east portion of the main floor. The hand-painted stage curtain on the second floor is a designated feature of the building.

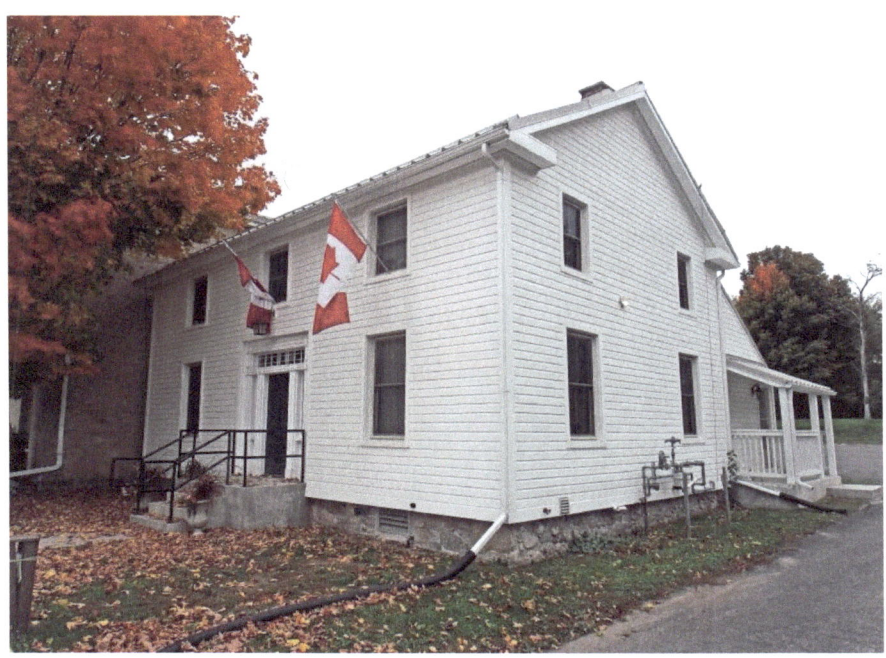

10836 County Road 2 - Township Hall Annex - Just east of the Township Building is a simple Neo-Classical house, now owned by the Township and used as office space. This house was built in 1860 by Scottish master carpenter John Aird. Although this building is clad in aluminum siding, the original clapboard remains intact beneath. Within the front porch is a fine Neo-classical doorway with delicate sidelights and transom fitted with original hardware. The walls of the house are plank construction.

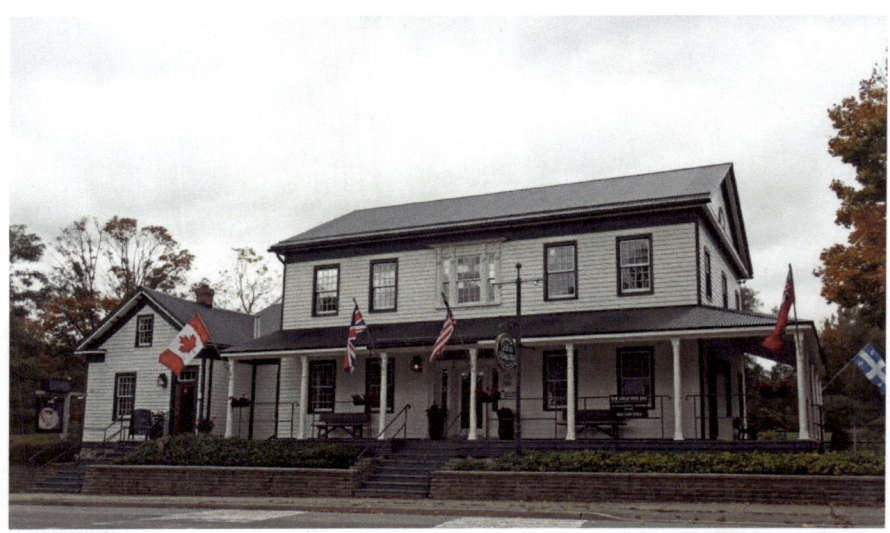

10830 County Road 2 - Grafton Village Inn was built in 1833 to replace a log building. The Neo-Classical building was restored in the early 1990s bringing it back to the early appearance that greeted travelers approaching from Kingston, York or Grafton Harbor. Its distinctive features include the front door surround with carved oak leaves and acorns, the second floor Venetian window and the demi-lune windows at each gable end. The western wing was a later addition and at one time housed the telephone exchange.

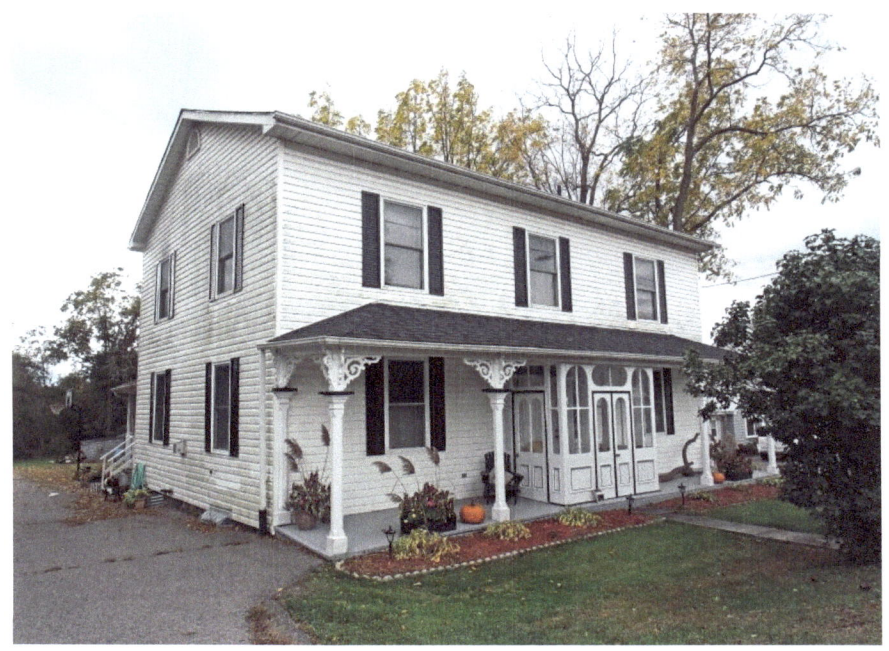

10799 County Road 2 - Church of England Rectory - two storey white clapboard house - Built in the early 1840's, the east side of this house originally faced the highway and was flanked by two wings. In 1849 it became the Church of England Rectory and in 1892 it was turned on its site and the wings removed. The distinctive Victorian veranda was added at that time.

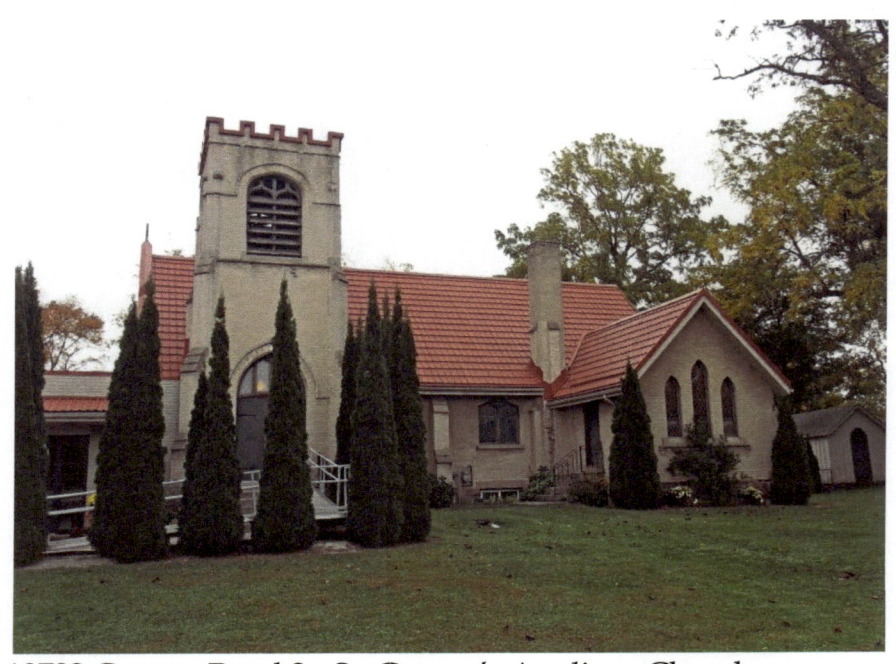

10792 County Road 2 - St. George's Anglican Church - formerly the Church of England - The original 1844 church was the first church building in Grafton. This early Church was dedicated by Reverend A.N. Bethune, an ancestor of Dr. Norman Bethune. Tragedy struck in April 1908 when fire destroyed the building. The new church was built in just ten months and, as so often happens in Grafton, a lot of help came from the other local churches. The style is English Ecclesiastic and has a tower with battlement and Gothic buttresses and windows.

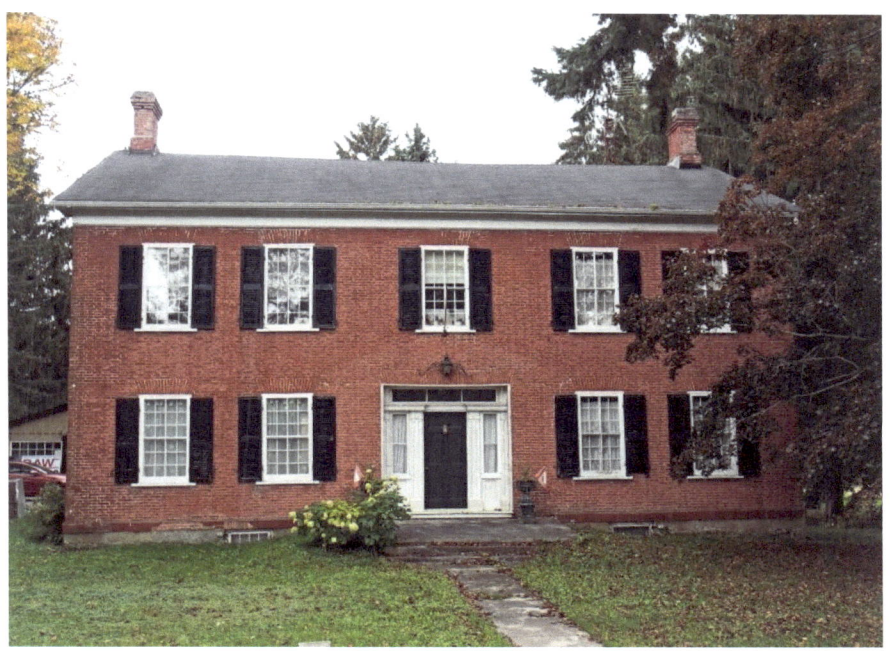

10715 Highway #2 - John and Mary Steele (nee Spalding) House is a handsome Georgian structure built by Thomas Spalding for his daughter Mary and her husband John Steele of Colborne. They moved here in 1843. The front door surround has several Neo-Classical features. Sections of the original brick are laid in Flemish bond. Over the years, deteriorating brick has been plastered over, painted and then stenciled to resemble brick.

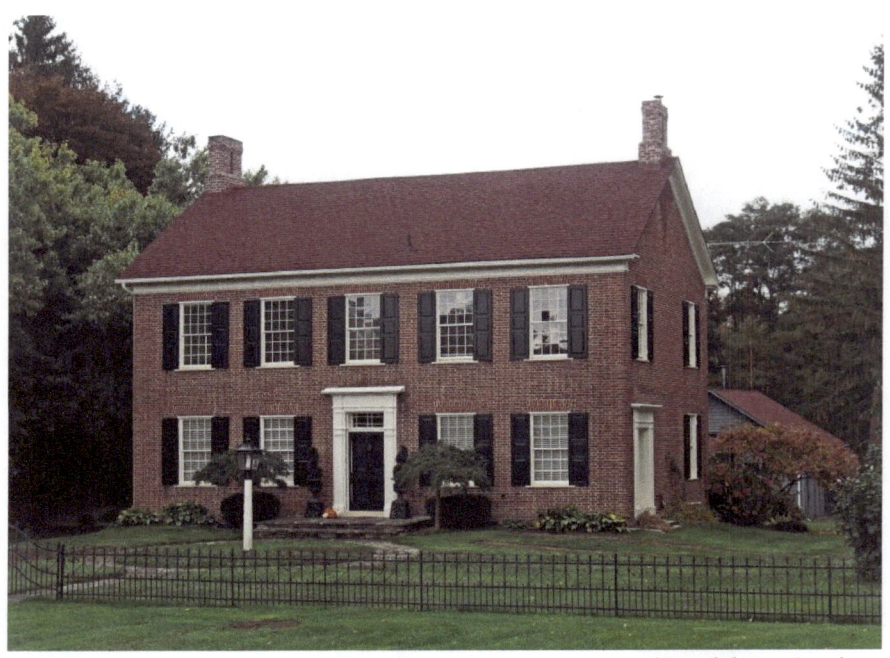

10701 Highway #2 - Thomas Spalding House (Spalding Inn) was the home of Thomas Spalding and was built in about 1835, probably of bricks made in his backyard on the property. Strong Georgian influence is evident in the transom door, balanced façade and inset chimneys atop this two-and-a-half storey dwelling. The mellow colored bricks are laid in Flemish bond.

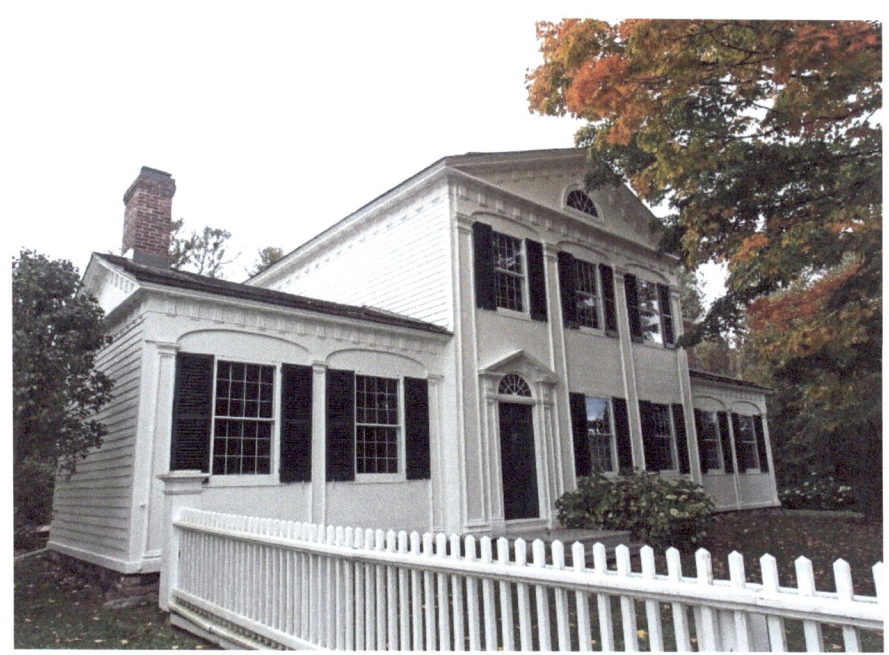

10568 County Road 2 - Barnum House (National Heritage Site of Canada) - The Barnum House was built between 1817 and 1819 by Eliakim Barnum, a United Empire Loyalist originally from Vermont. The house which stands just outside Grafton is the earliest example of Neo-Classical architecture in Canada. Barnum House was the first house museum to open in Ontario, restored and operated by the Architectural Conservancy of Ontario in 1940. In designing his house, Eliakim Barnum was influenced by American Architecture, popular in New England states at the beginning of the nineteenth century. This Neo-Classical style was intended to reproduce elements of classical Greek architecture. These include a central temple front with flanking wings, articulation of the façade with pilaster linked by elliptical arches, and extensive use of delicately scaled details. The Neo-Classical elements of the house's exterior are echoed in the ornate woodwork of several interior rooms.

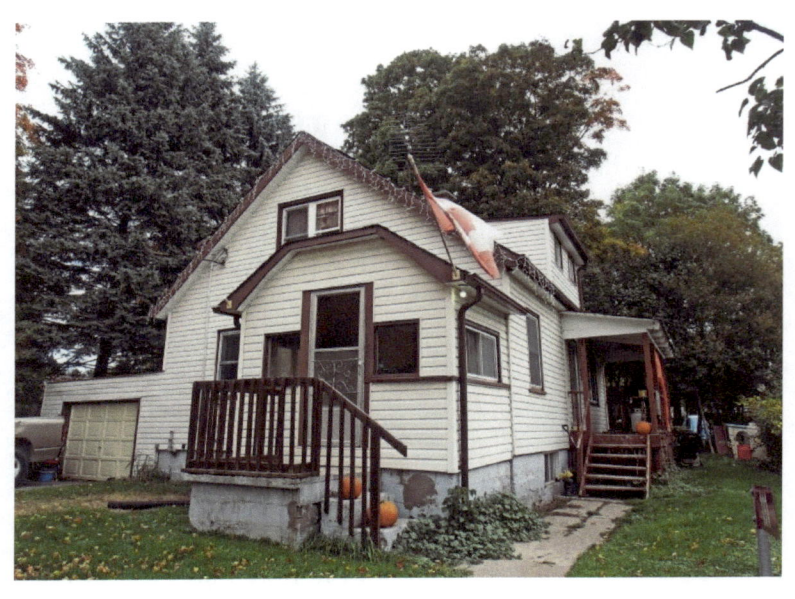

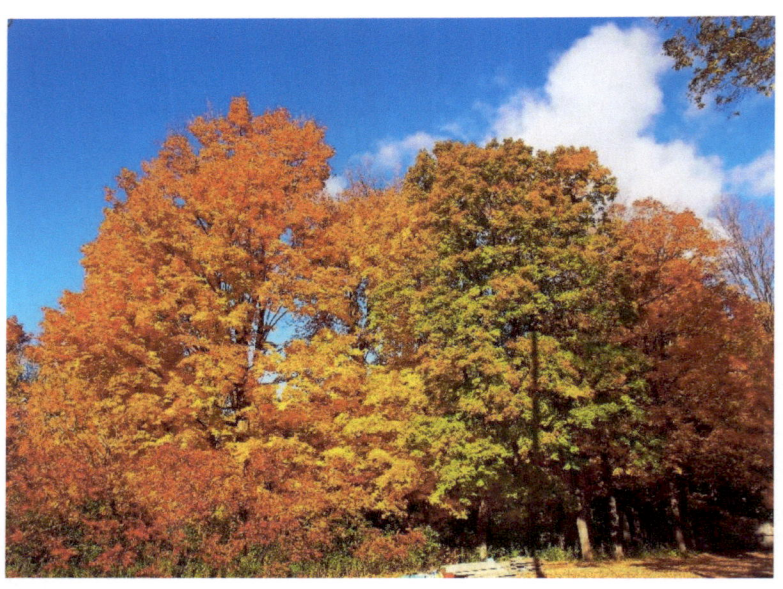

Bolton

Mature black walnut trees grace Nancy Street.

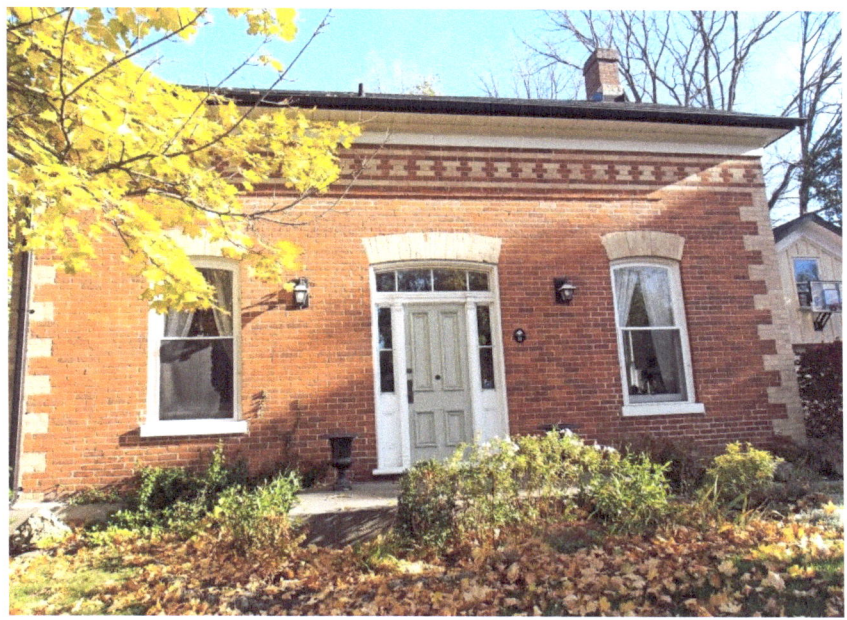

11 Nancy Street - Dr. Stewart House - circa 1887 - This Neoclassical style house with its beautiful doorway was built using local red and yellow brick by George Watson for Dr. Robert L. Stewart.

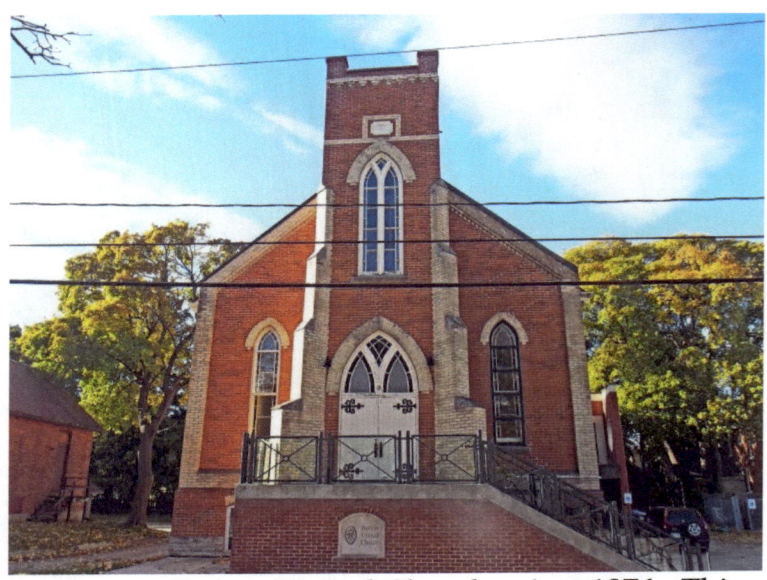

8 Nancy Street - Bolton United Church - circa 1876 - This Victorian Gothic style brick church was built by George Watson for the Wesleyan Methodists. After church union in 1925, it became Bolton United Church. For safety, the original spire was removed in the 1930s. A Sunday school wing was added in 1978.

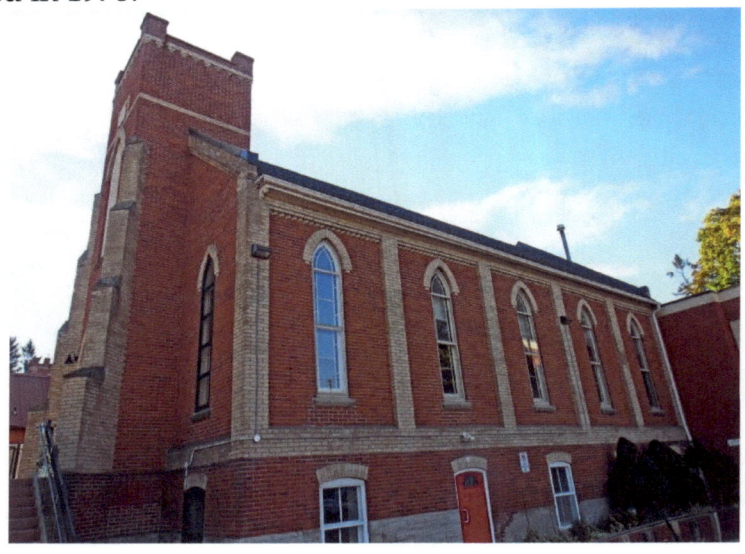

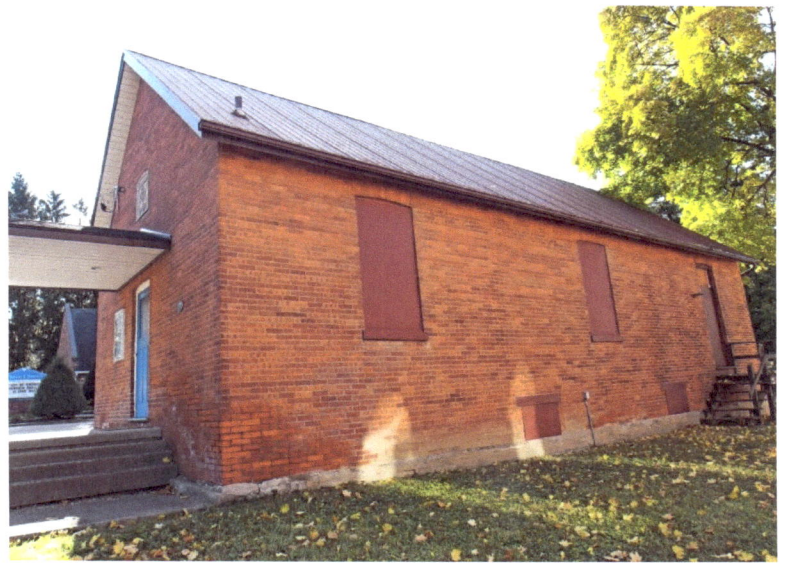

16 Nancy Street - Masonic Hall - circa 1876 - Members of True Blue Lodge #98 built this frame building. In 1889, they added beautiful carved furniture and improved the interior. In 1894, the building was raised for a new foundation and basement. Brick cladding was added in 1903.

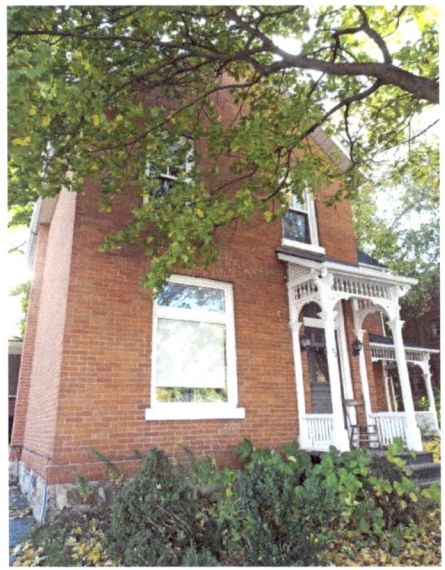

54 Nancy Street

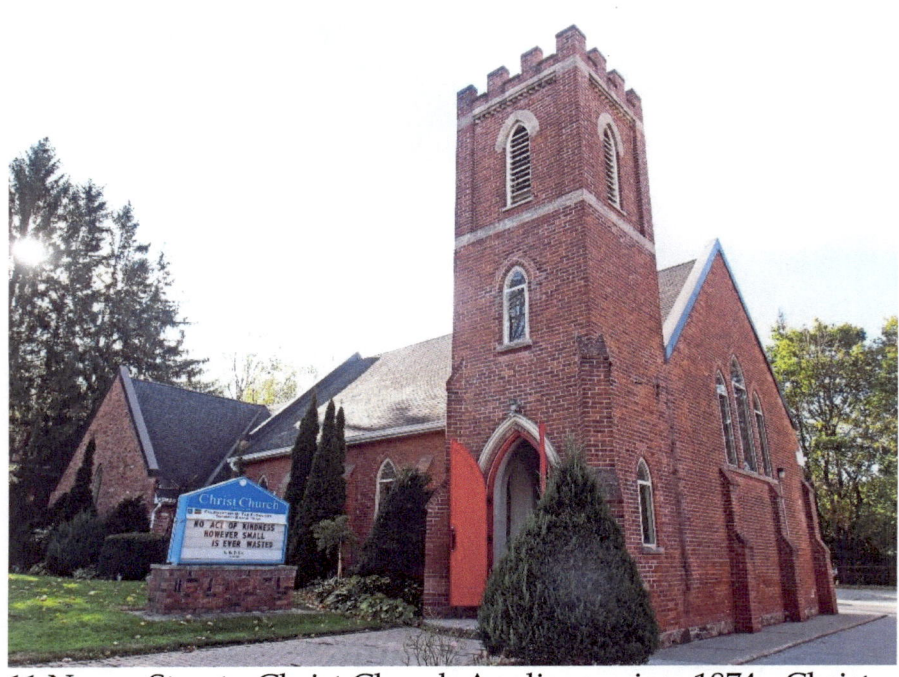

11 Nancy Street - Christ Church Anglican - circa 1874 - Christ Church was built on property donated by James Stork, a local seed and grain merchant. Nancy Street was named after his daughter. The brick church replaced earlier mud-brick and frame structures. Since 1874, the church has undergone several renovations, including the 1959 parish hall addition. When the Sanctuary was enlarged in 1986, the original bricks from Norton's brickyard were re-used on the extended wall facing the street.

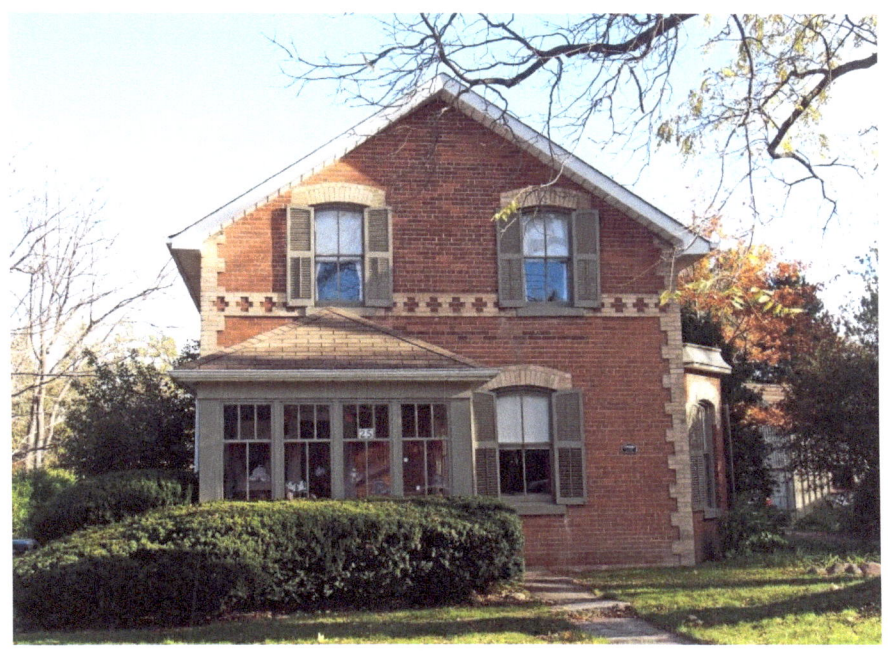

25 Nancy Street - Alice Goodfellow House - circa 1884 - This 1½ storey Victorian Gothic home was built by George Watson for Alice Goodfellow using local red and yellow brick. The end gable patterning and the enclosed front porch are excellent examples of late nineteenth century urban architecture. Alice's sister Margaret Smith lived next door. On Alice's death in 1901, her brother-in-law Albion farmer James Goodfellow and his wife Marion retired here. It was in their family until the owner of 31 Nancy Street purchased it in 1999.

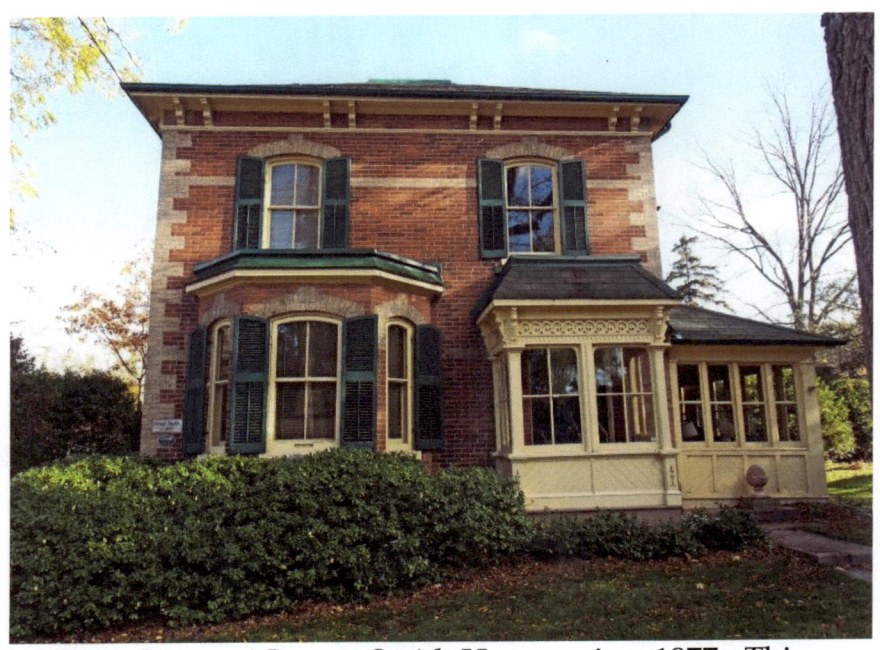

31 Nancy Street - *George Smith House - circa 1877 - This Italianate style home was built by George Watson for Margaret and George Smith. The red and yellow bricks were locally made and its exterior architectural features and beautiful enclosed porches are original. Smith, a sign painter and letterer, sat on the first village Council and was noted for his very realistic interior faux-wood graining. Erie Smith Schaefer inherited the house in 1933, living here with her husband Alex of 'Smith & Schaefer' Hardware. This dichromatic brick house is in the Italianate style. The orientation of the 'L' plan with the enclosed verandah along the south is distinctive. The bracketed eaves, segmentally arched windows and low medium pitch hipped roof are all typical of the Italianate.

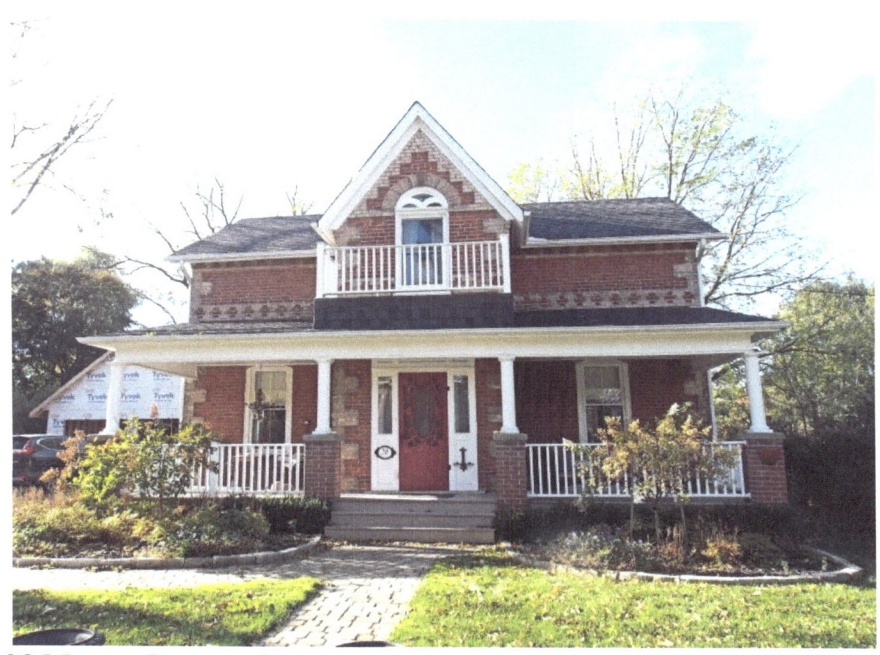

38 Nancy Street - George Watson House - circa 1873 -This seven room Victorian Gothic brick house, with its long front verandah, was built by George Watson in a cross-like shape which gave all main floor rooms three exterior walls. Watson, wife Margaret Bell, and children Minnie, Eva and Fredrick lived here until 1888 when it was purchased by the Methodist congregation as manse.

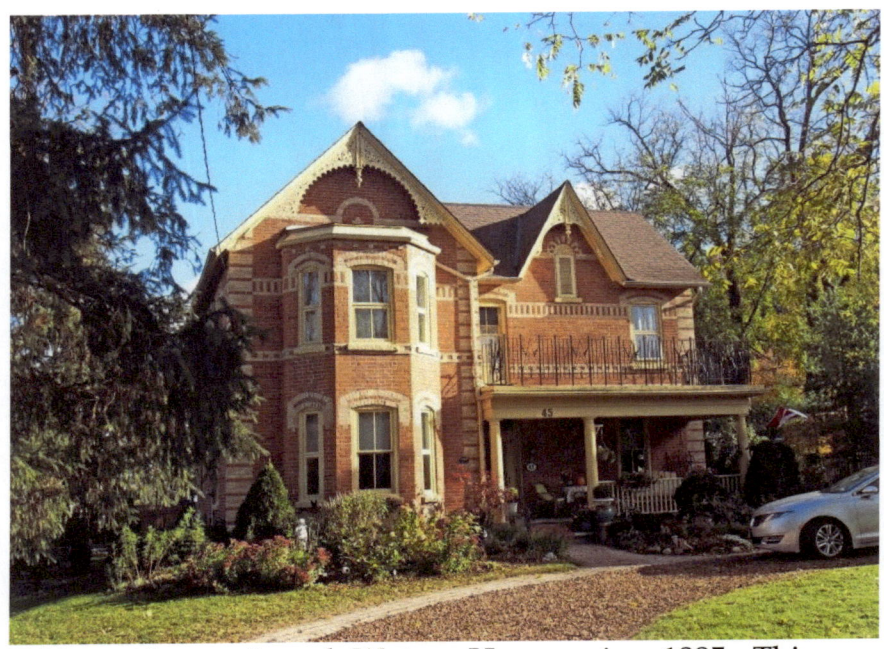

45 Nancy Street - Joseph Watson House - circa 1885 - This Victorian Gothic style house was built by George Watson for his older brother Joseph, who retired to Bolton in 1888 from farming/carpentering in King Township. The house displays a higher degree of detailing than others of this style with elaborate patterned fretwork, drop finials and patterning created with the local red and yellow brick. It has a two-storey bay, ornate brick patterning, and verandah and gable scrollwork.

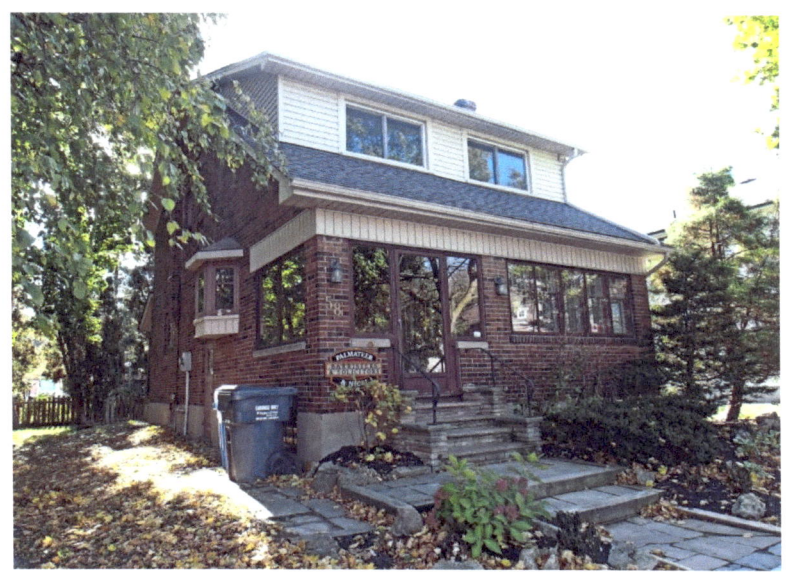

58 Nancy Street

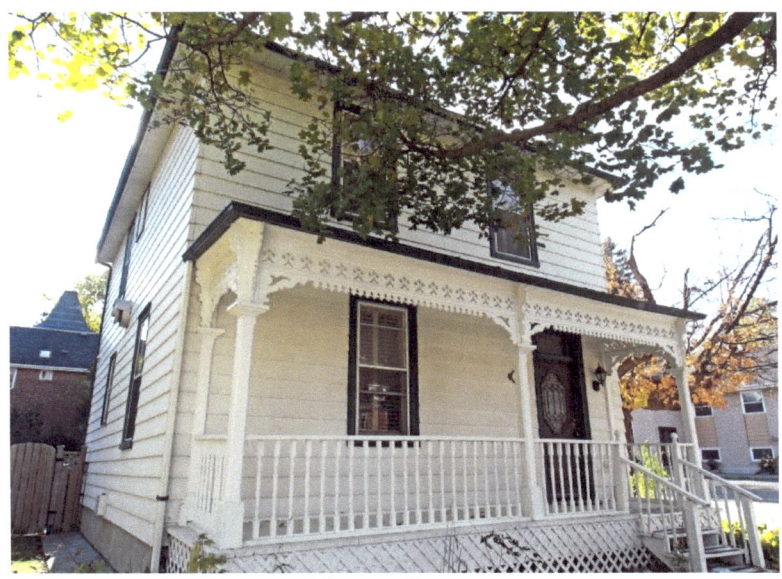

Nancy Street

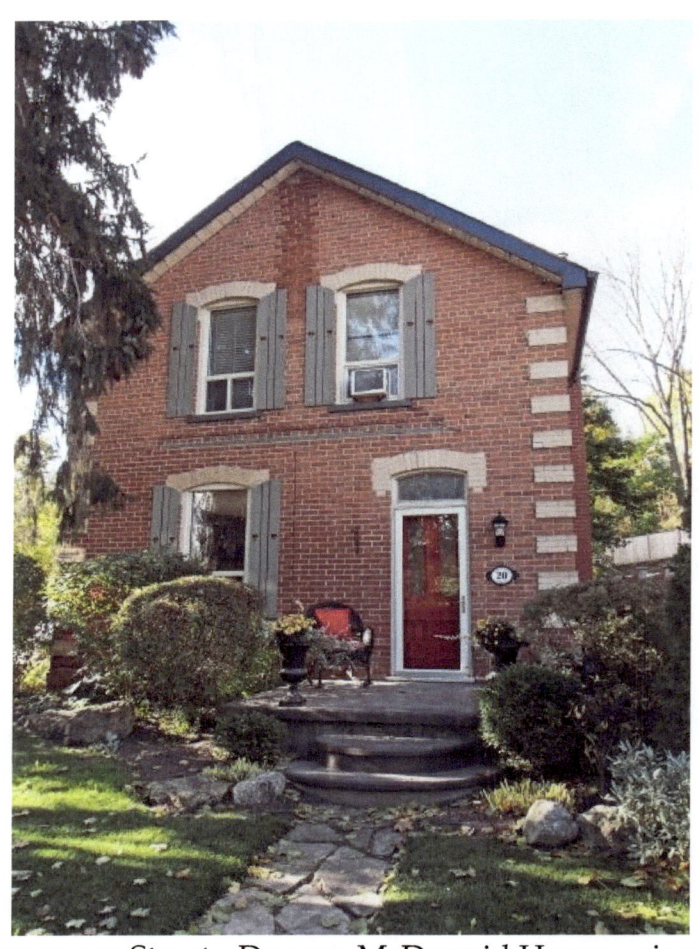

20 Temperance Street - Duncan McDermid House - circa 1885 - This 1½ storey Victorian Gothic house, with its detailed red and yellow brick patterning was built for Duncan McDermid by Henry Shore. It originally had a highly decorative front verandah. It was later sold to coal and lumber merchant, village councillor John Arnott in 1909. In 1931 Elsie Hardwick bought it. Her son Otto managed Bolton's first pasteurizing plant. BA oil dealer Eldred and Hilda Camplin bought it in 1952.

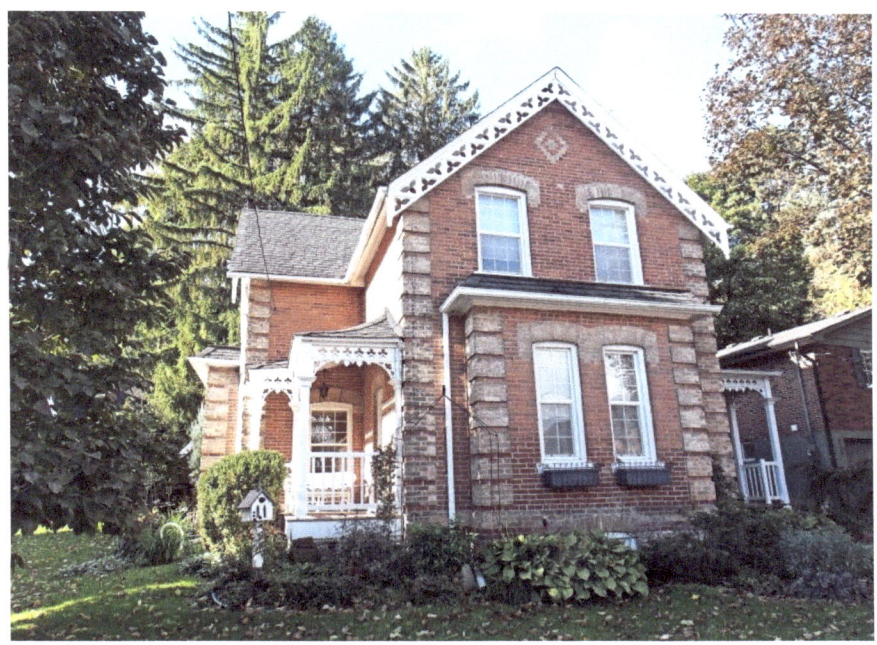

34 Temperance Street - Shore-Nease House - circa 1872 - This Victorian Gothic house was built by Henry Shore using red and yellow brick in a style typical of an urban village setting. The trillium patterned fretwork on the decorated wooden porch has been repeated on adjacent buildings. From 1892-1969, it served as office and surgery to Bolton doctors, including Dr. Lepper, Dr. A. Jackson, Dr. Graham and Dr. Taylor. The building is a fine example of a polychromatic brick 'L' plan residence featuring a diamond pattern at the gable of each section with accents of quoins and arches, and an 'L' form verandah formed at the inside corner between the two sections.

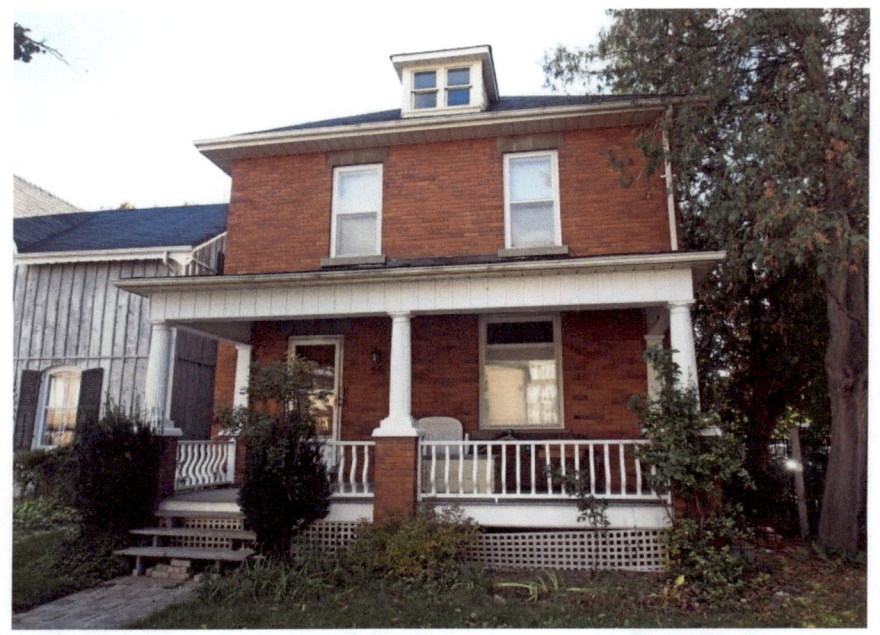

56 Sterne Street - circa 1900 - This 'four square' red brick house is built in the Edwardian Classical style, characterized by an asymmetric floor plan, attic dormer window, full front verandah with classical column supports and pyramidal hipped roof. For many years into the 1960s, it was the home of Mrs. Alice Goodfellow and her twin sister Miss Monkman.

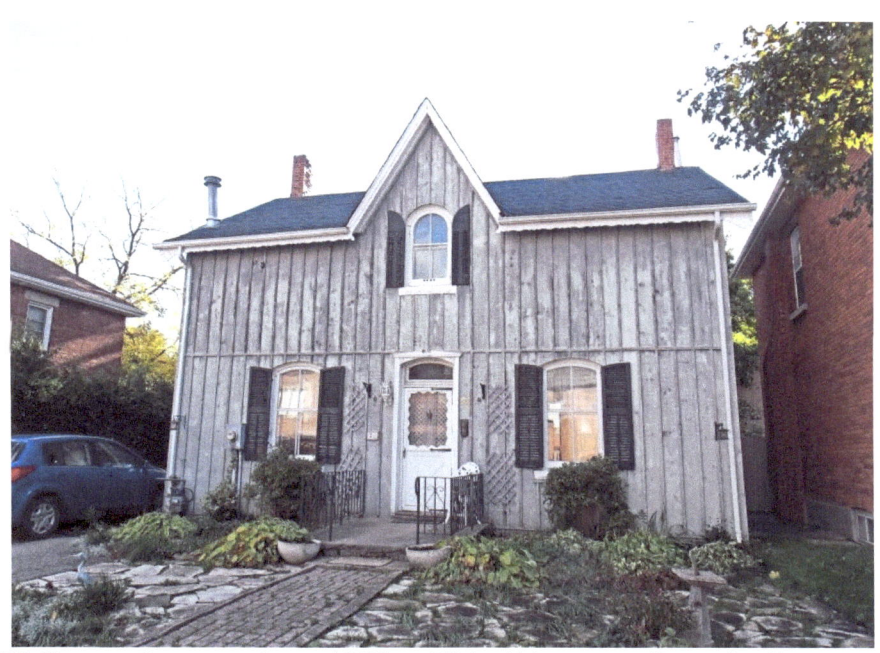

52 Sterne Street - circa 1870s - This 1½ storey Ontario Cottage has the characteristic centre entry flanked by symmetric windows and arched window in the centre gable. The exterior is clad in wood. The shutters appear to be original and are functional rather than merely decorative. There is clear etched glass in the transom light over the door.

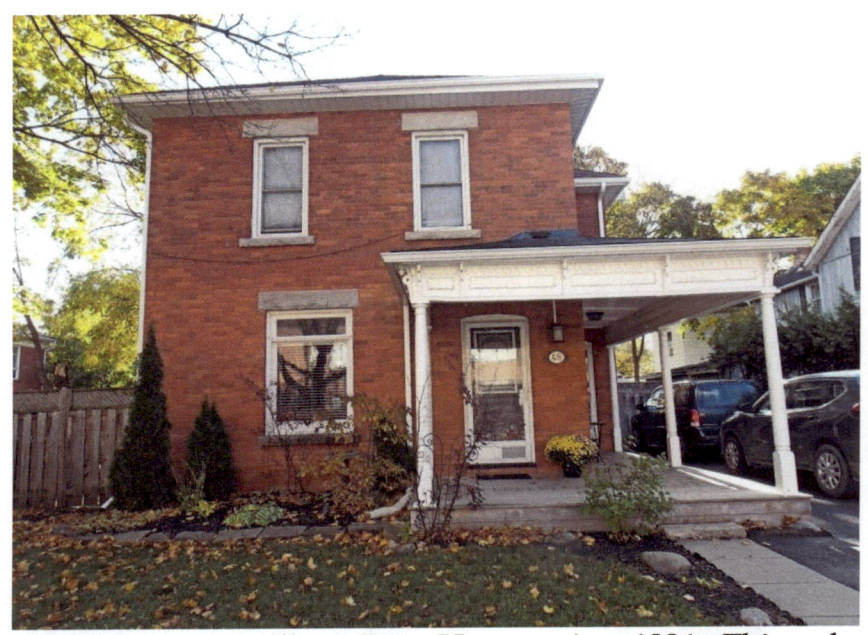

48 Sterne Street - William Buist House - circa 1884 - This red brick Edwardian Classical style house was likely built by George Watson for William Buist, who moved here after selling the saw and woollen mills in Glasgow which he and his brother had operated for twenty years. Buist retired in 1906 and sold the house to George Nunn who was an agent selling Heintzman pianos, sewing machines and Dominion & Bell organs. There is turned woodwork on the wraparound verandah and there is limestone trim.

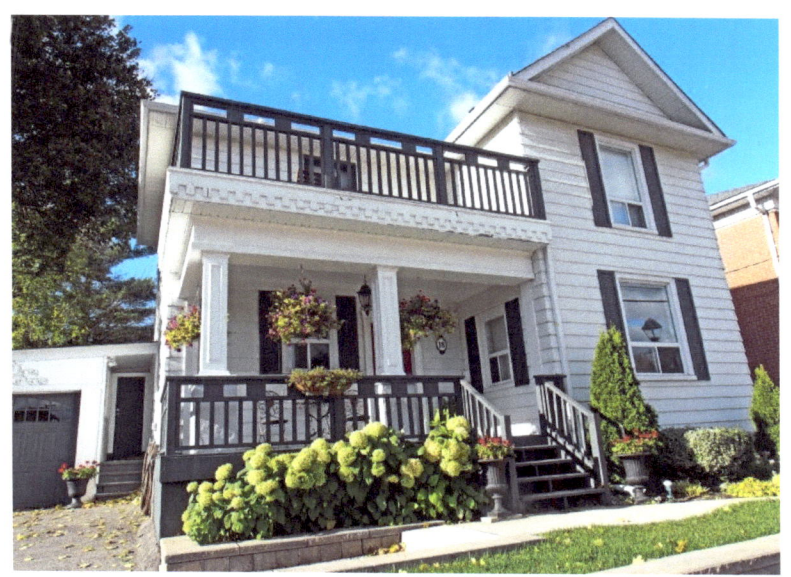

18 Sterne Street

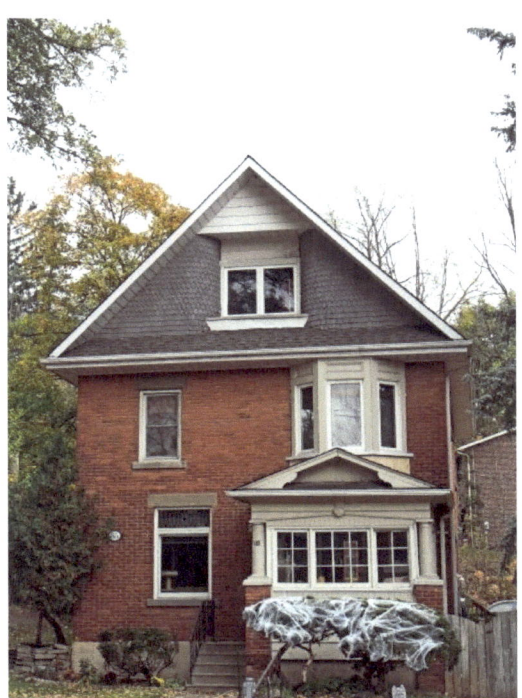

85 King Street West

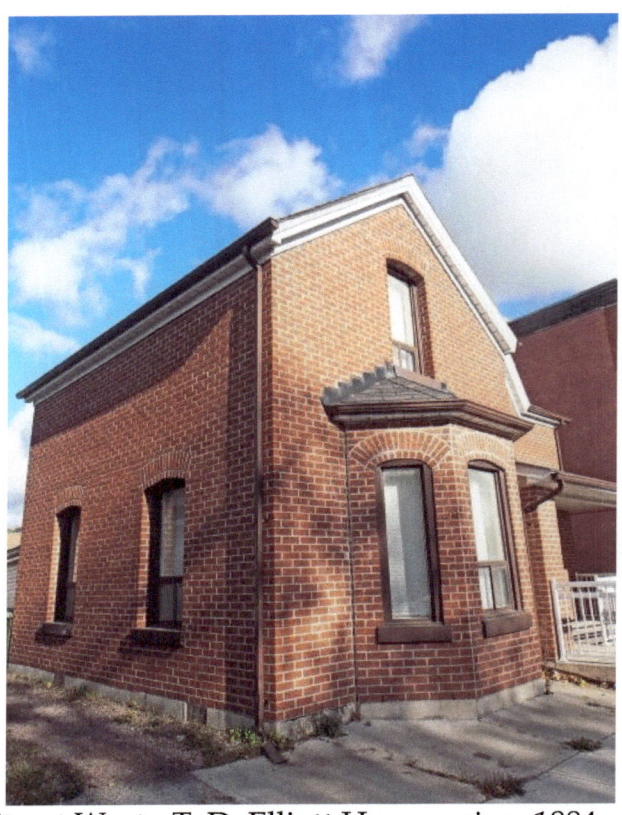

11 King Street West - T. D. Elliott House - circa 1884 - This Victorian Gothic house was built by George Watson using local red brick with yellow brick trim for Thomas D. Elliott's marriage to Helen Evans, daughter of 'Squire' George Evans, Queens Hotel owner and local magistrate. T.D. became Innkeeper, managing all hotel operations including stables and the successful stud business. Later, son Elwyn 'Jacky' and his wife Eulalia Potter lived here until Eulalia's death in the 1990s. The house was re-bricked in 2008.

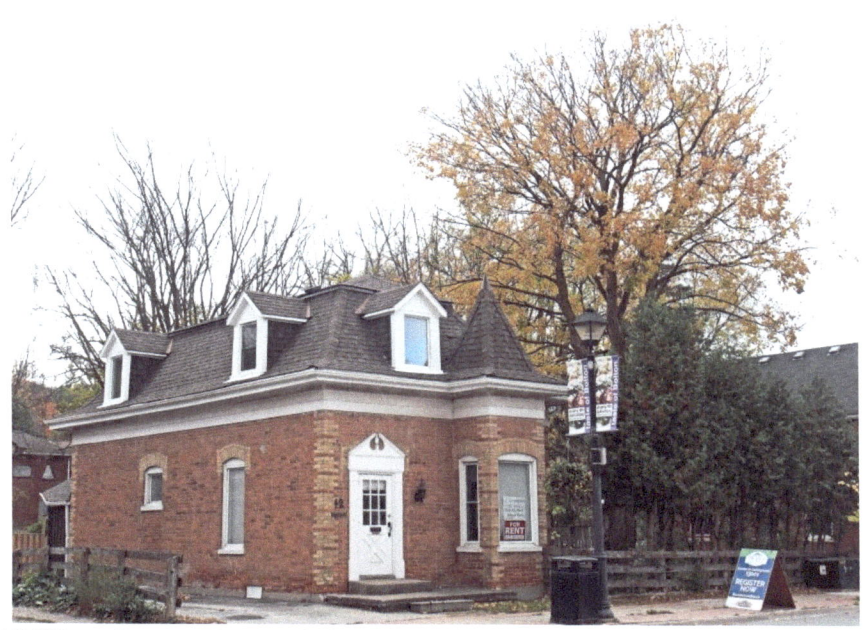

12 King Street West - 'The Castle' - mid-1870s - A rare example of the Second Empire style with its mansard roof and square projecting bay, this house was built for Ann Roberts. Ownership passed to her son William L. Roberts in 1893 and from him to Margaret Jane Osburn in 1907. Olga and Wesley Strong and their son Charlie lived here until 1923 when Wes's health failed. Charlie lived to 100 and was a great Bolton story teller. Mrs. Dickson owned the house in the 1930s and left it to her daughter Pearl who raised eight children here with her husband Lee Morrison.

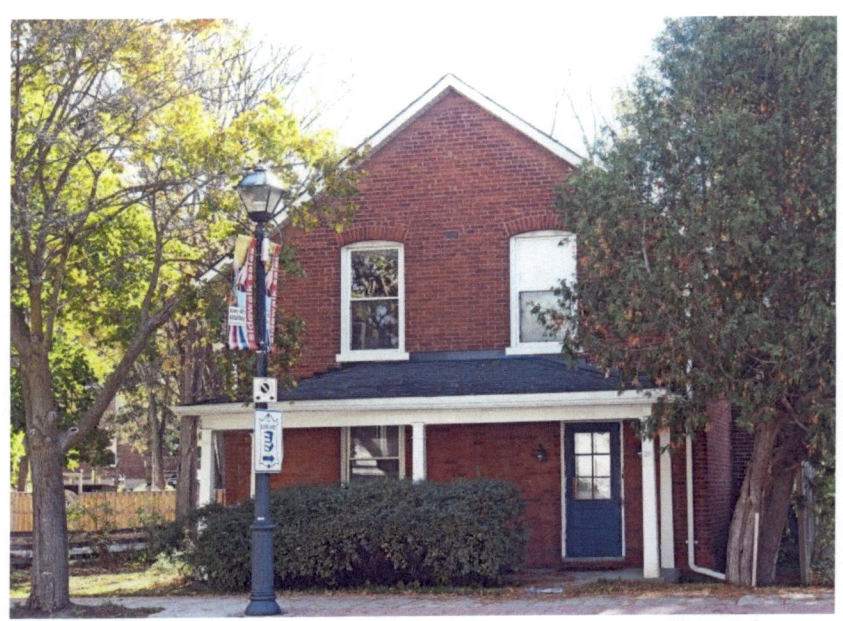

20 King Street West - Banks House - pre-1891 - Albion-born Ann Jane Corless and her husband Alexander Banks and their four children lived in this red brick Victorian Gothic house from the late 1880s until they moved to Toronto around 1910. Daniel and Alice Henderson, also born in Albion, were married in 1902 and moved into the house in 1914. Dan worked for Beamish Butchers for some 50 years. Daughter Olive, a member of the women's 1925 All- Ontario softball championship team, lived here until 1997.

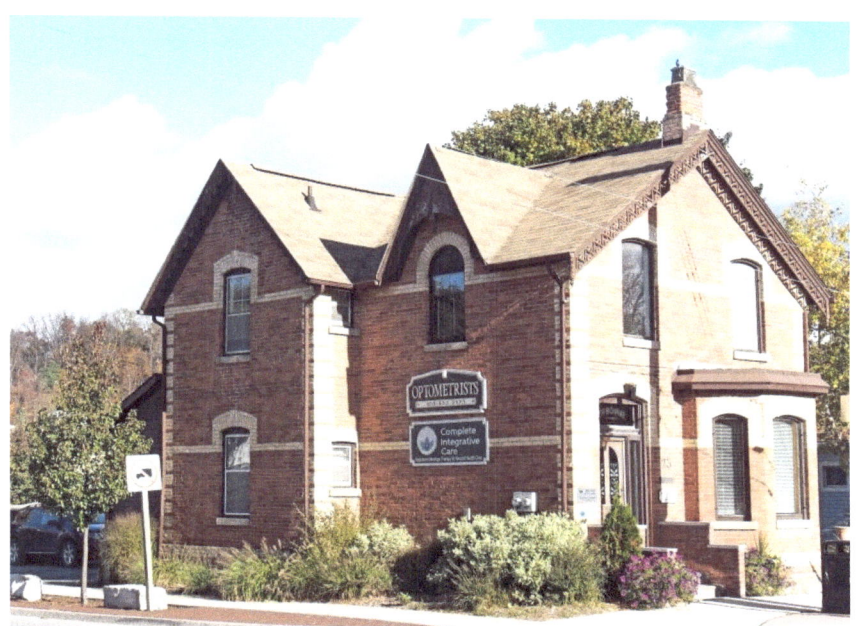

23 King Street West - Dr. Bonnar House - circa 1884 - Dr. Bonnar and his wife Margaret came to Bolton in 1870. George Watson built this red and yellow brick Victorian Gothic office-residence. Dr. Bonnar's name is etched in the transom glass above the front door. He served on the village Council, School Board, Library Board and Cemetery Board, and was coroner of Peel County for many years. The Bonnars' daughter Mrs. Mary Frampton lived here until 1952.

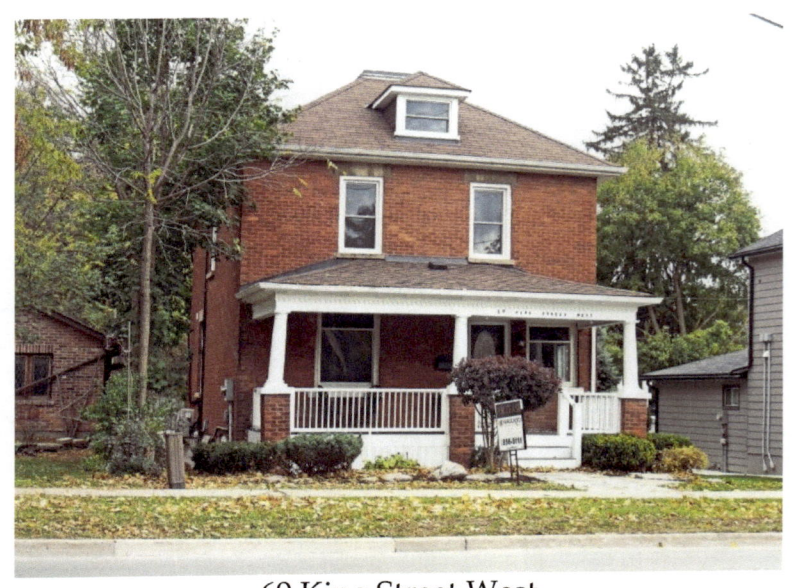
69 King Street West

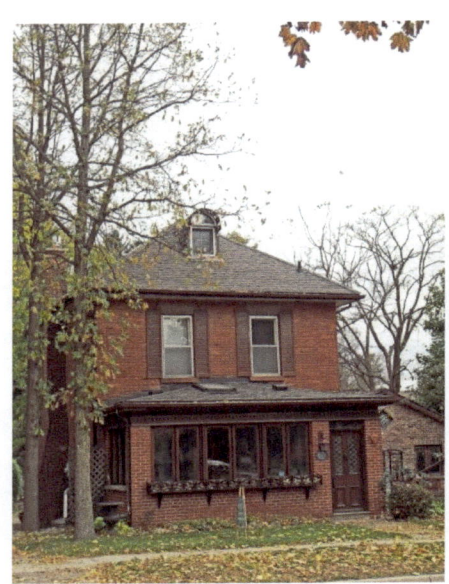
75 King Street West

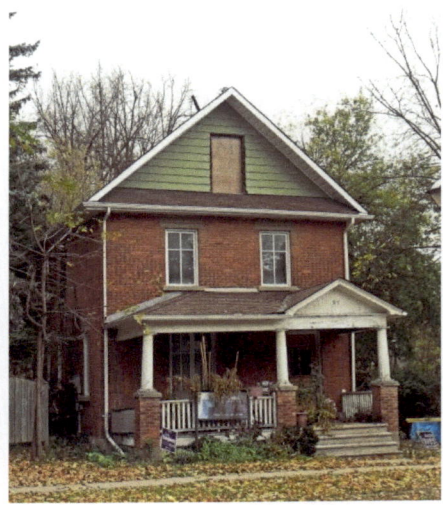
81 King Street West

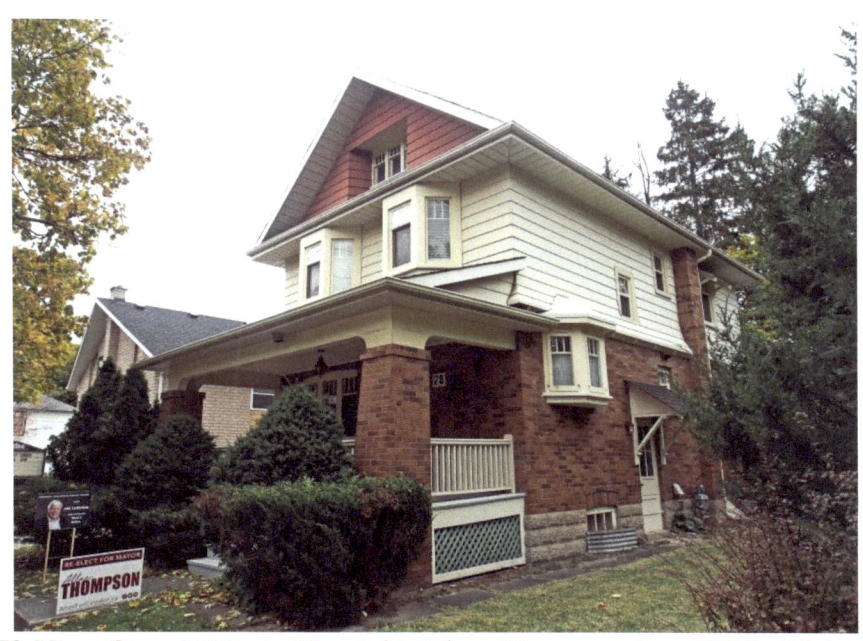

78 King Street West - Daniel Mabee House - circa 1920 - This Edwardian Classical style house with its characteristic asymmetric floor plan and prominent verandah was built by Bill Black for Daniel Mabee, who operated the corner grocery store at King/Queen Streets. In 1929, Mabee sold it to William Westlake, Agricultural Society President who in turn sold it to Thomas Keyes in 1942. Harold Egan, partner in the Egan Funeral Home and Egan Brothers' Store, and his wife Mary lived here from 1947 to 1971.

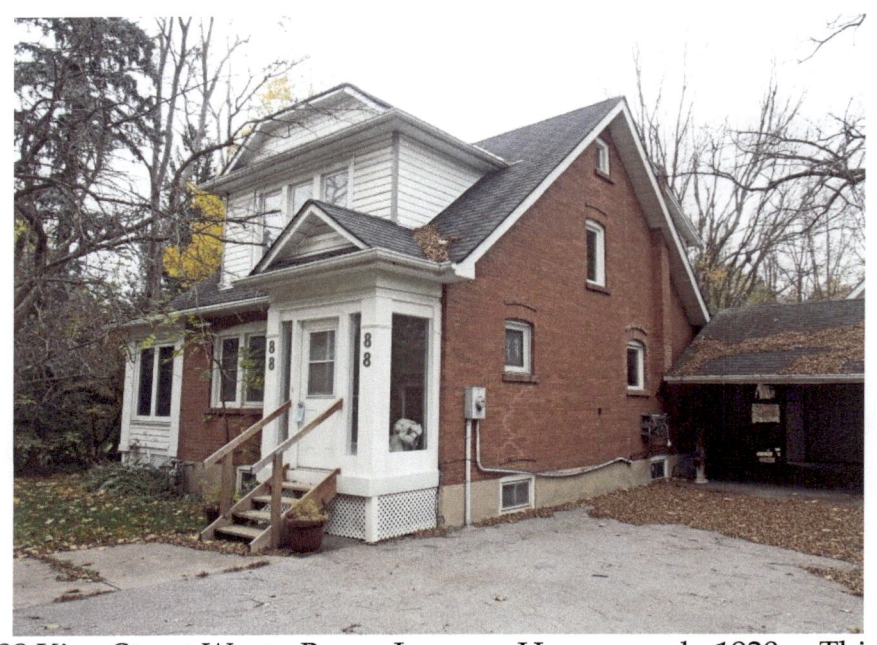

88 King Street West - Byron Leavens House - early 1920s - This 1½ storey brick Craftsman style bungalow was built for Byron Leavens, son of 'The Enterprise' owner Frank Leavens. Leavens served in France in World War 1 and as Postmaster in Bolton from 1927 until 1945. He had just built a new post office building at 29 Queen Street North when he died unexpectedly. His wife Mary became Postmistress until 1947 and she remained here until the house was sold to the current owners in the early 1960s.

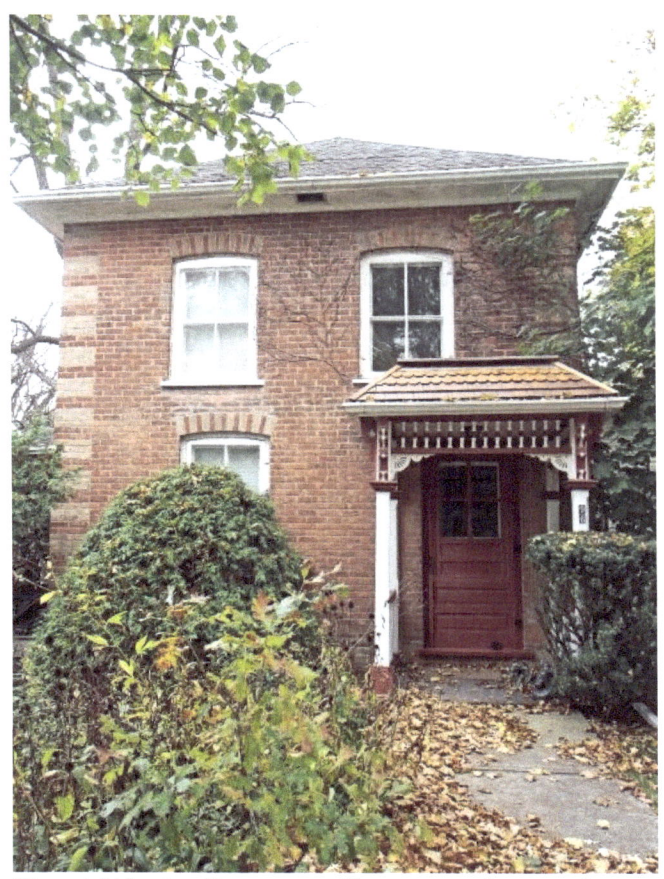

96 King Street West - Coventry Cottage - date unknown - This house was reportedly built as a cottage in the nearby hamlet of Coventry, later moved here and placed on a new foundation. While the addition on the west side is recent, the carefully restored wood shingled front porch with decorative trim is original to the house.

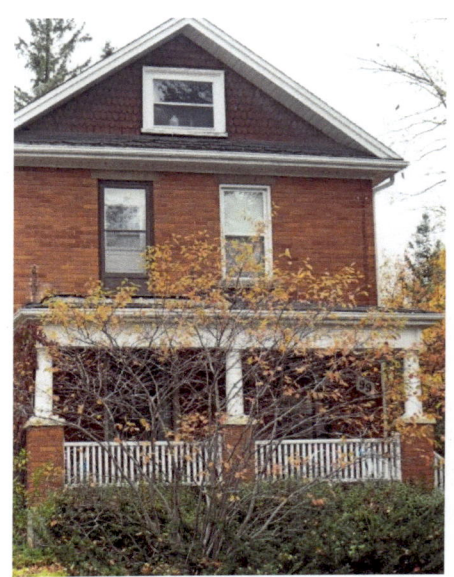

99 King Street West

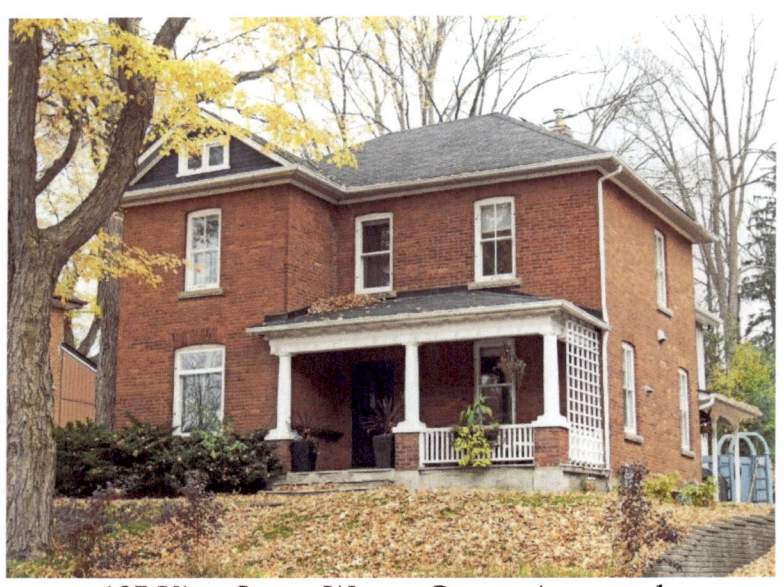

105 King Street West – Queen Anne style

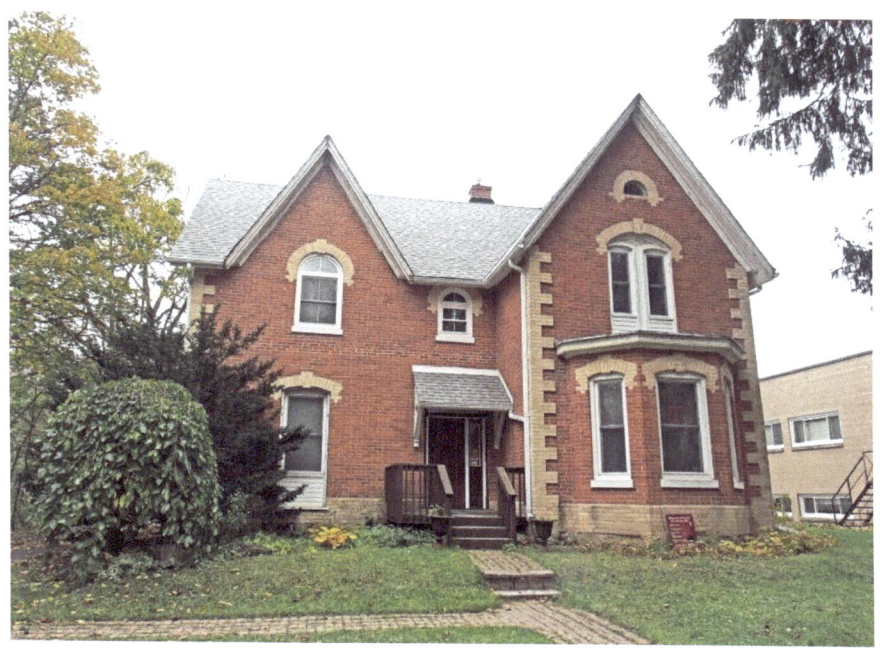

102 King Street West - Presbyterian Manse - circa 1885 - This large Victorian Gothic home was built by George Watson for the Presbyterian minister and family. The red and yellow brick used in the house is local from Norton's Brickyard. Jaffary's Creek runs behind the house.

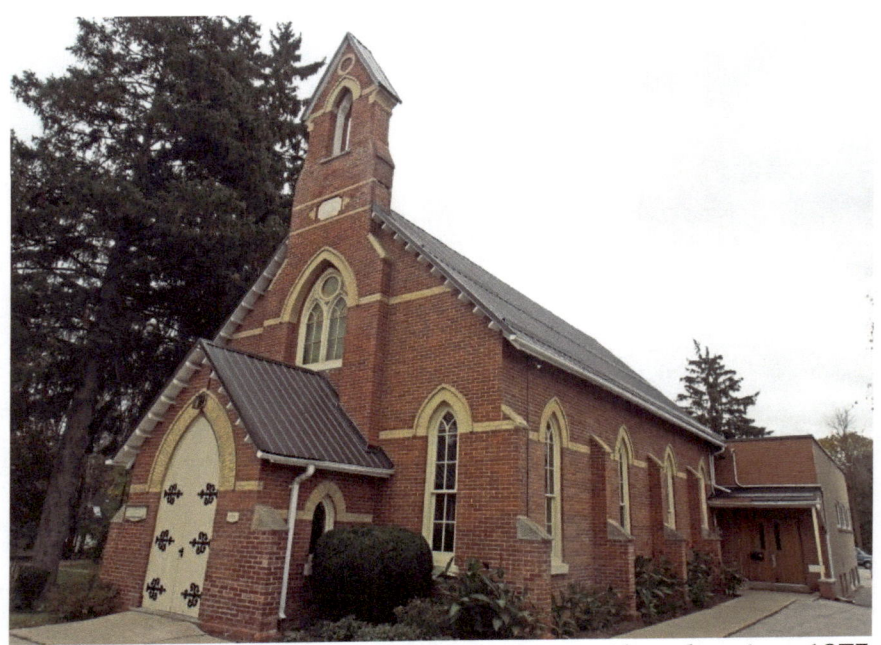

110 King street West - Caven Presbyterian Church - circa 1875 - This landmark Victorian Gothic church was built in 1875 by George Watson, Master Builder. The inaugural service was conducted by Reverend Caven, Principal of Knox College at the University of Toronto, after whom the church was named. The red and yellow brick is local from Norton's Brickyard.

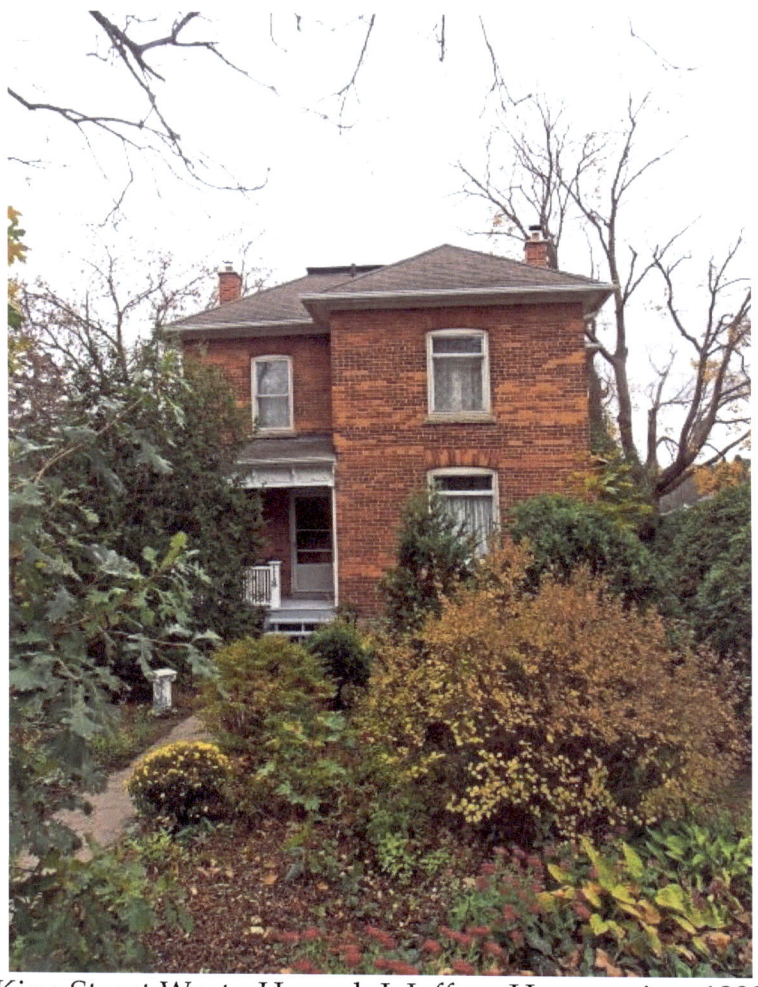

118 King Street West - Hannah J. Jaffary House - circa 1900 - This Edwardian Classical red brick house was the first house built by Bill Black in Bolton. It was owned by Wyatt Jaffary's daughter Hannah. Jaffary's Creek, named after Hannah's family, runs behind it.

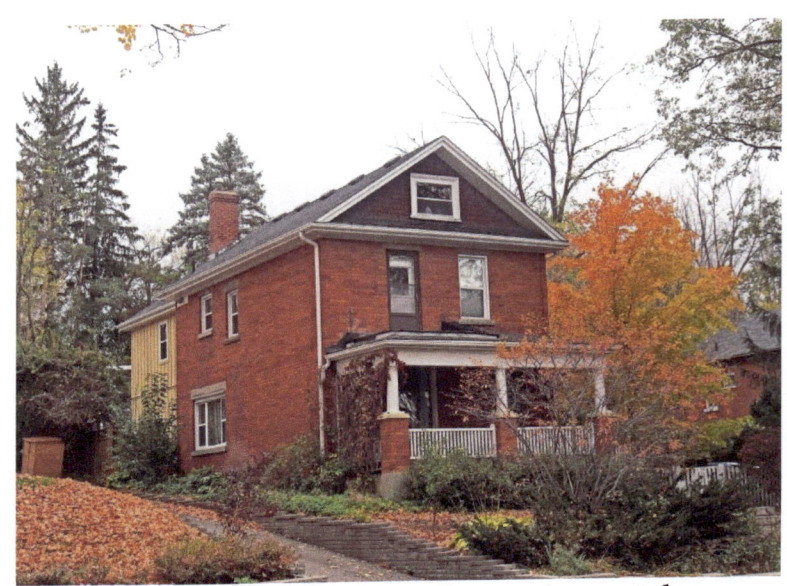
113 King Street West – Queen Anne style

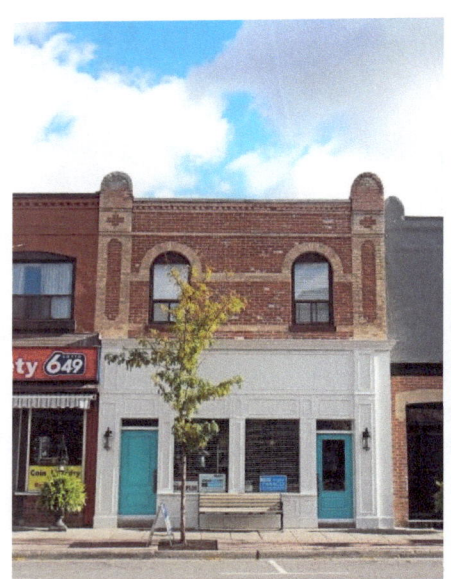
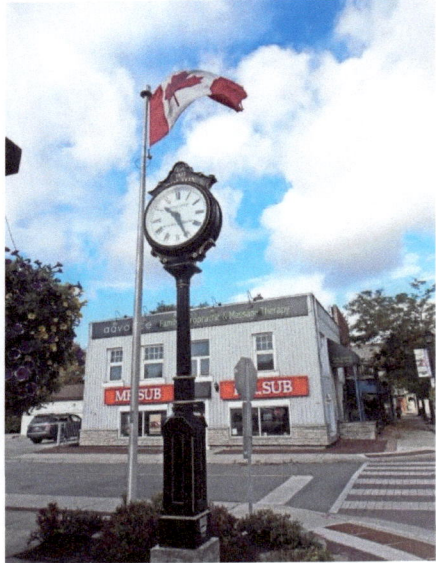
Queen Street North

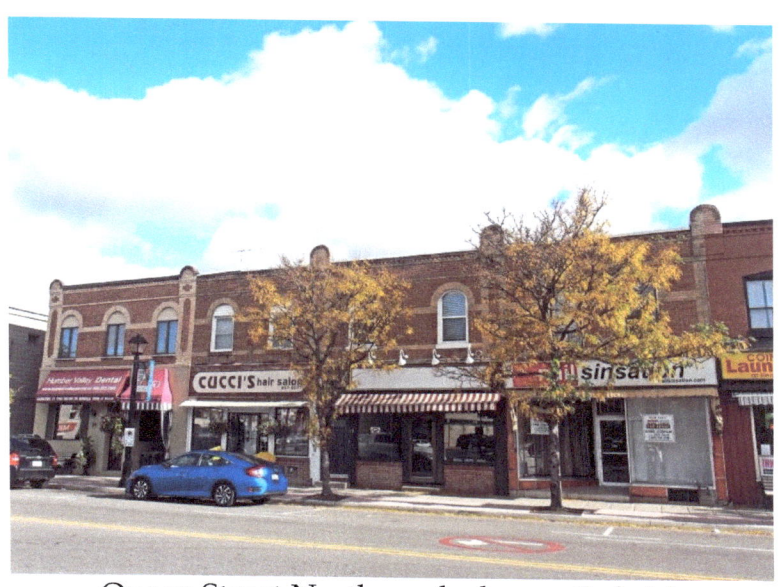
Queen Street North - polychromatic brick

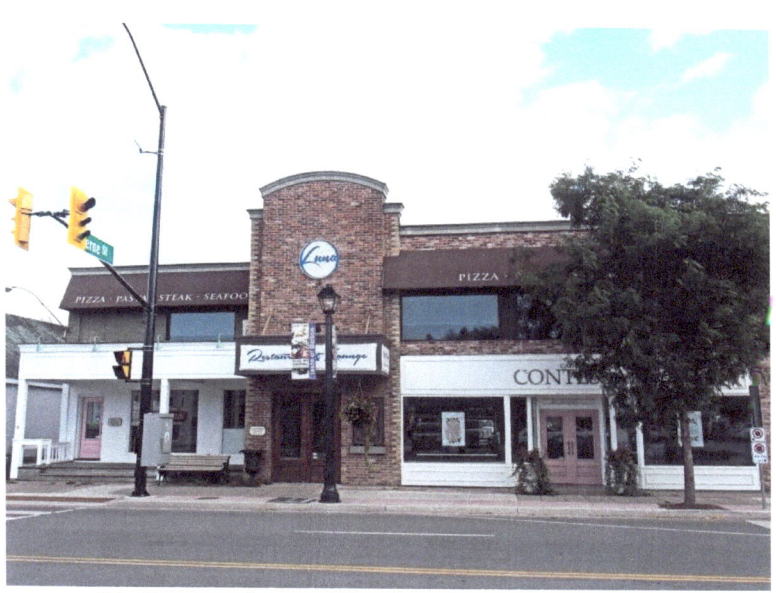
31 Queen Street North – Luna Restaurant

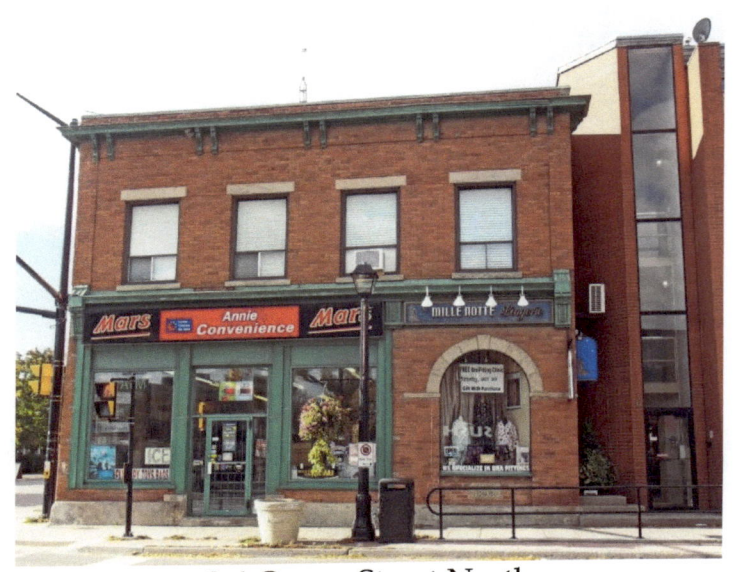

2-4 Queen Street North

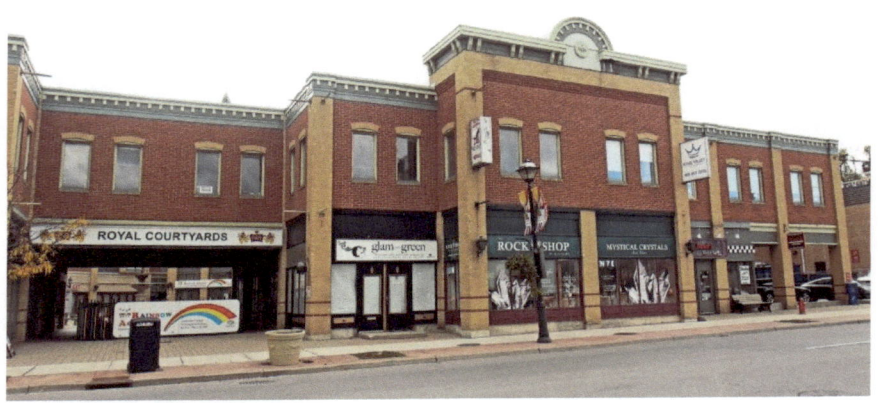

18 King Street East – Royal Courtyards - 1989

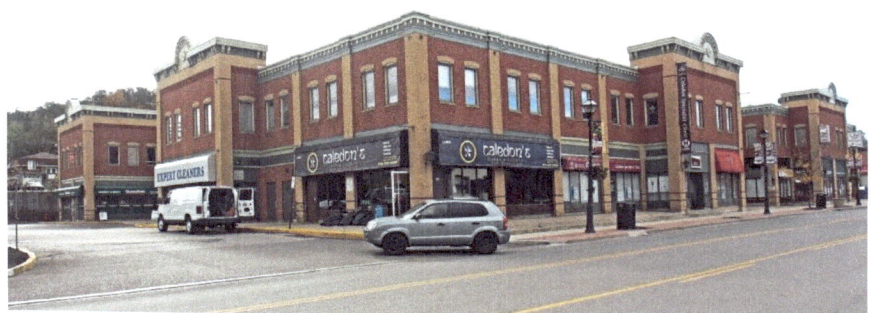

The Royal Courtyards - circa 1988-89 - This urban mall was built with red brick and yellow brick trim, replicating the look of brick structures built a hundred years earlier. Jaffarey's Creek is contained in concrete culverts underneath the Royal Courtyards from where it flows into the Humber River below the McFall Dam.

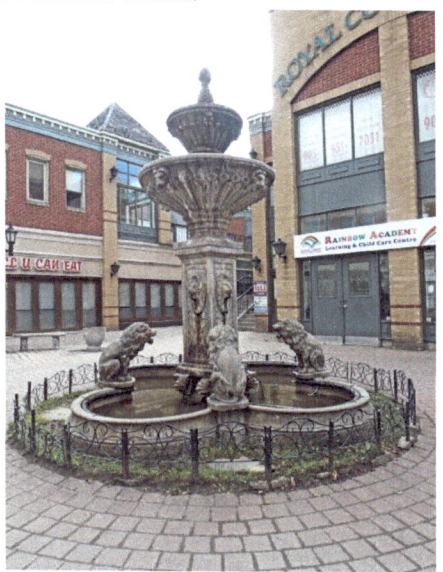
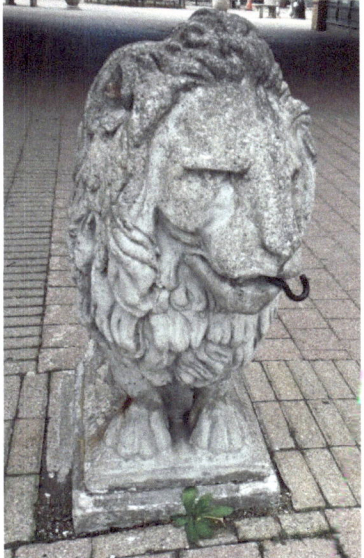

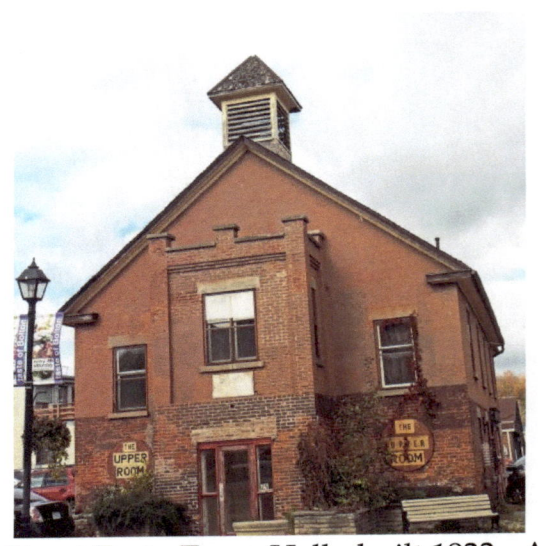

15 King Street East - Town Hall - built 1922 - After fire destroyed Bolton's village hall in 1920, this new town hall was erected on the same site. The lower level comprised the village council chambers and library, while the upper level was an auditorium for concerts, clubs, Guide meetings and dances. It acted as village fire hall. Space was rented to a furniture and casket maker.

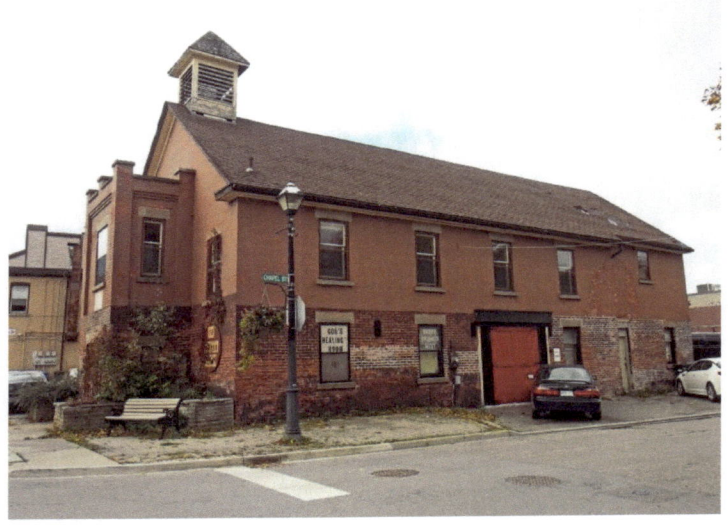

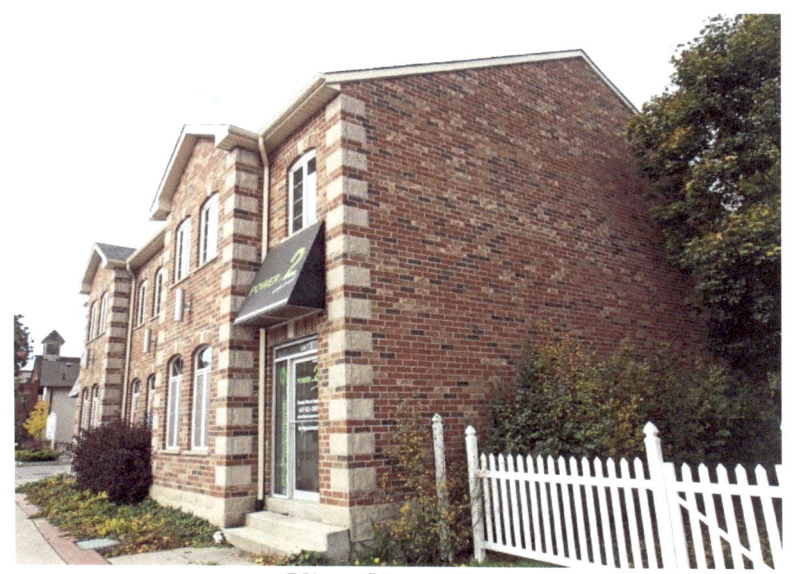

King Street East

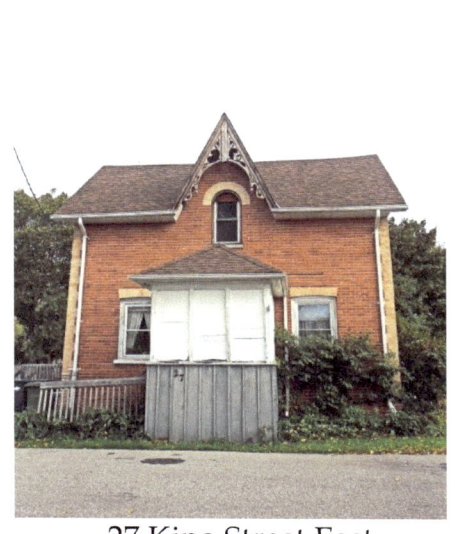

27 King Street East

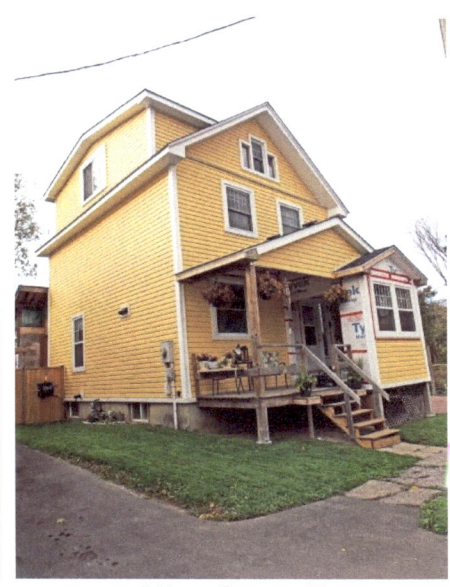

King Street East

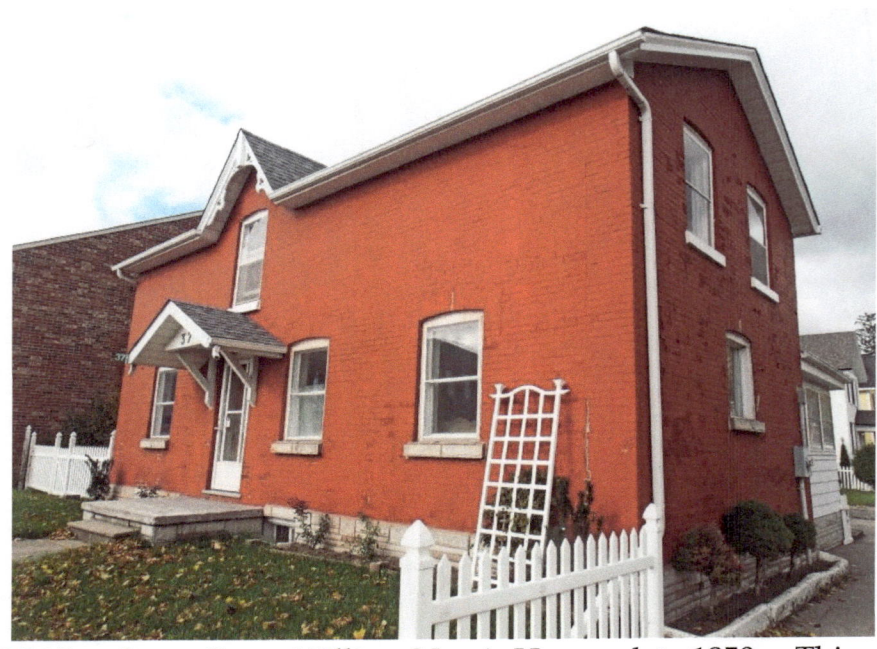

37 King Street East - William Norris House - late 1850s - This frame Ontario Cottage with picket fence was purchased by William Norris in 1864. He built a store addition to the east side with a separate door and window to the street. Originally clad in roughcast plaster, it was later veneered in red brick with yellow brick trim, and decorated with ornate door stoop, carved posts and cast iron railing, all of which have been painted over or replaced. It was bought in 1910 by Alderman D.B Kennedy, Bolton Hydro and school board member who eliminated the separate store by converting its door to a window. John and Vera Elliott Goulter bought the house in 1953 and lived here for 60 years.

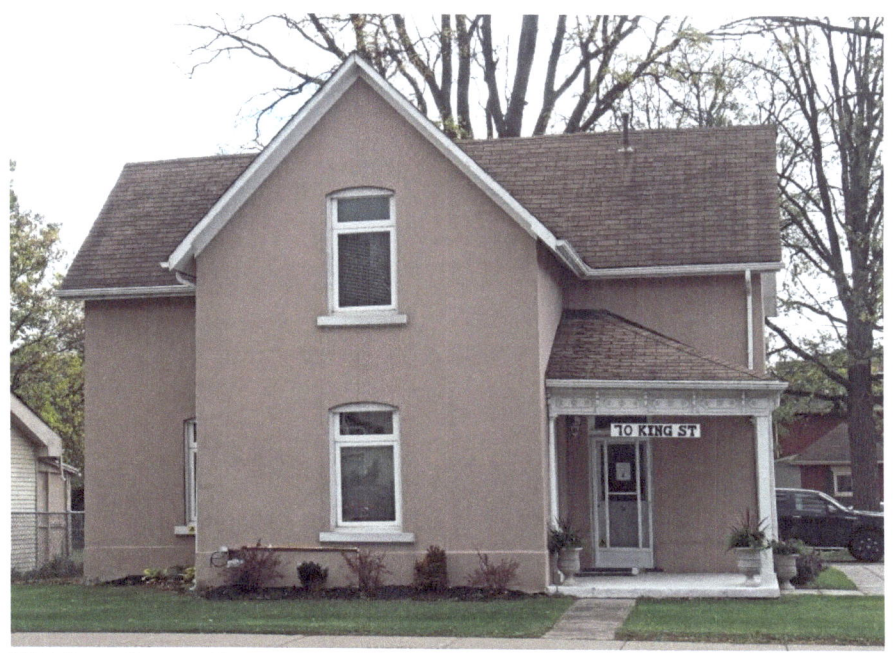

70 King Street East - Samuel Bolton House - circa 1849 - After the 1837 Mackenzie Rebellion, Samuel Bolton, nephew of George Bolton, fled from Albion Township to the USA with his father, James Charles Bolton, who died in Indiana (1782-1840). Later pardoned, Sam, a finishing carpenter and undertaker, returned to Bolton in 1845 and built this cross-shaped Victorian Gothic frame house for his wife Sophia Nunn. Sam built in wall niches which he used to display coffins. The house remained among Bolton and Fuller family members for a century, then in the ownership of the East family for another 50 years. Originally clad in roughcast plaster, the exterior is now stucco.

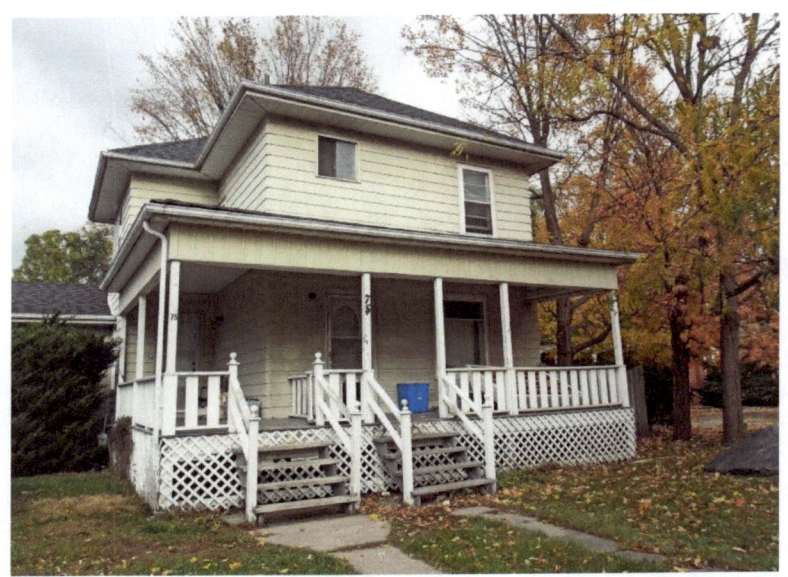

75 King Street East - Edwardian Classical House - late 1890s - This frame house was built on what was originally the 1840s creamery property. After WWII, it was owned for a number of years by Fergus Healey, who operated the creamery.

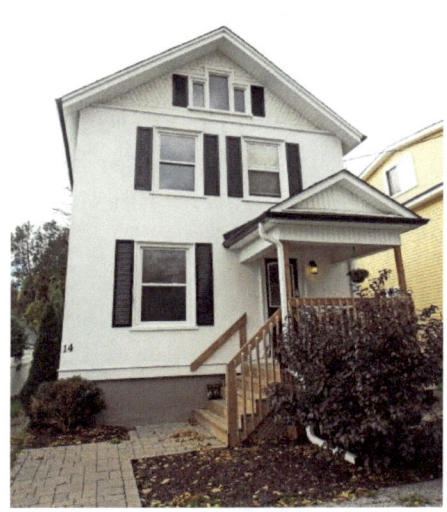

14 King Street East

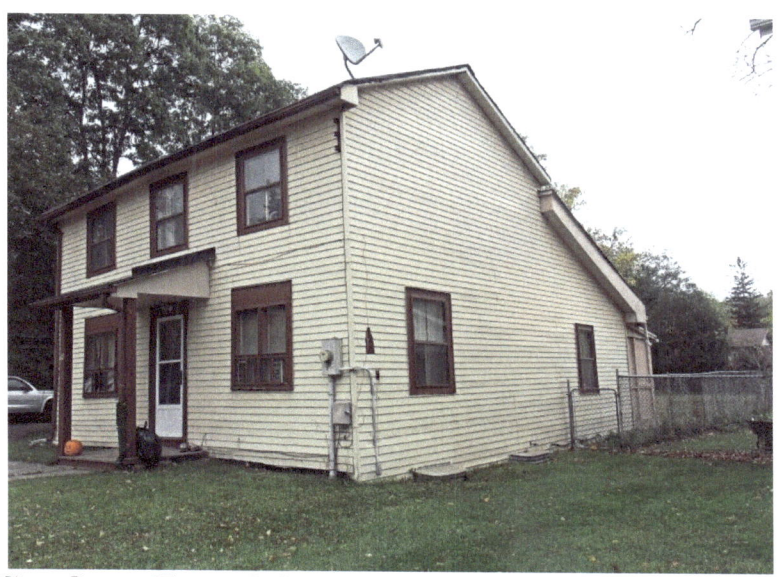

74 King Street East - Cabinet Maker's House - circa 1846 - William Hughes, age 22, built this two-storey, Neo-Classical style house. The saw mill down the street supplied the materials. It remains the earliest frame house standing in Bolton. Hughes, who specialized in cabinetry and chair making, lived in it with wife Jane and family until 1884. It then housed mill workers until Sarah Lundy and Harry Sheardown bought it in 1891, living in it for 43 years. Harry first worked in Dick's Foundry, later owned a barber shop on Queen Street North and was considered one of Canada's best all-round athletes.

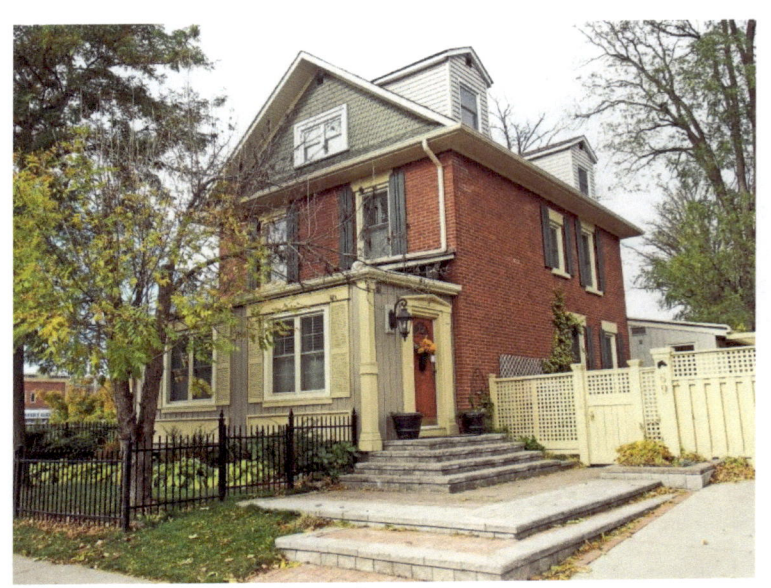

69 Willow Street

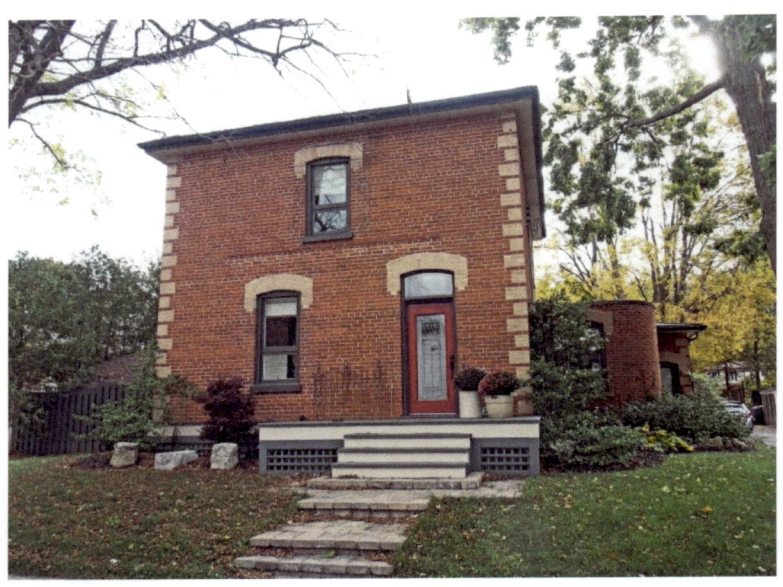

Sandhill

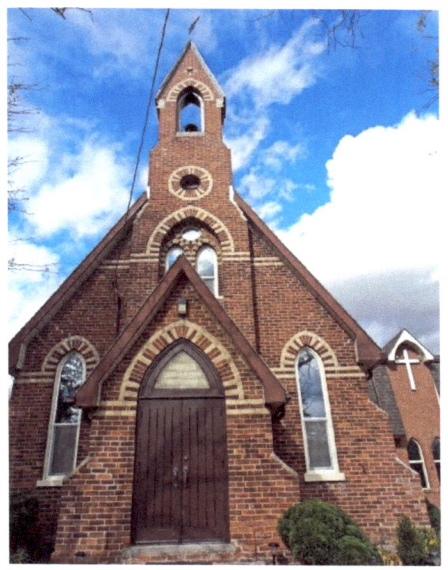

6060 King Street East, Caledon - North Peel Community Church – also called Shiloh Apostolic Church

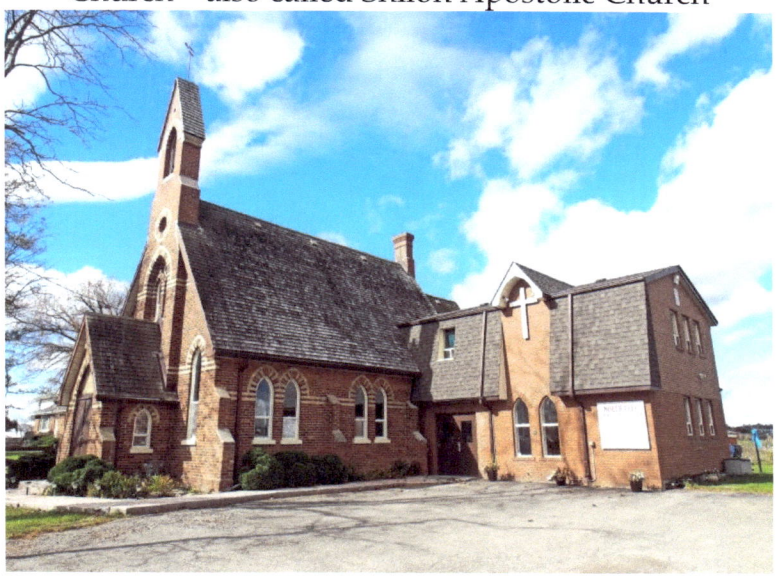

Campbell's Cross

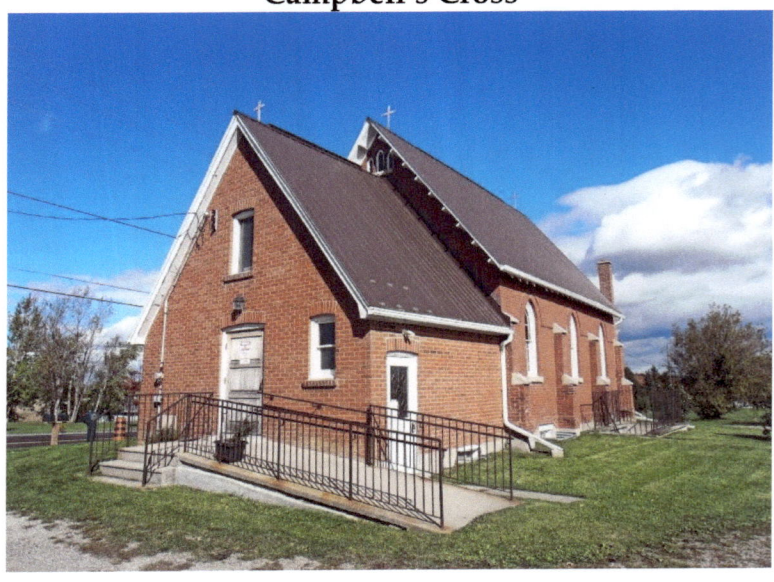

#3515 - May 30, 1899

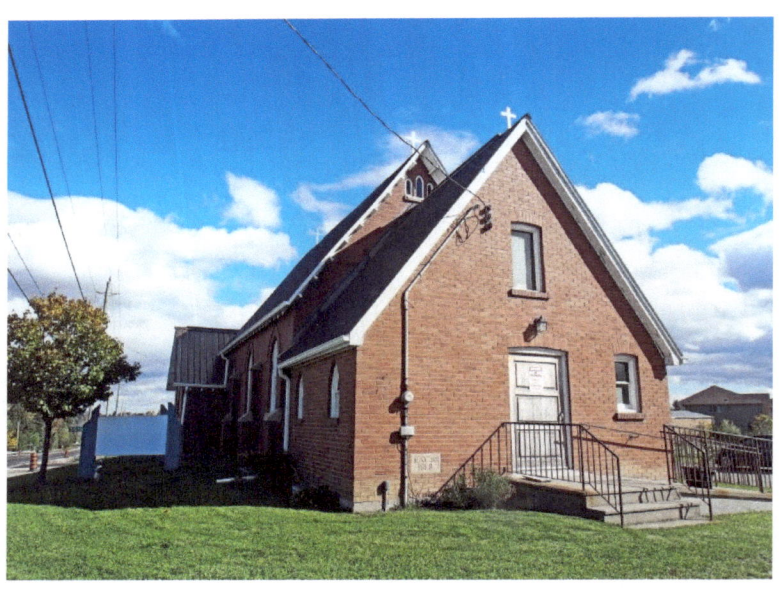

Other Books by Barbara Raue

Coins of Gold
Arrows, Indians and Love
The Life and Times of Barbara
The Cromwell Family Book
Laura Secord Discovered
Daddy Where Are You?

Montana Series
Book 1: Montana Dream
Book 2: Life on the Montana Frontier
Book 3: Montana to Boston and Back
Book 4: Montana Sons Go to War
Book 5: Montana Sons Return from War

Visit Barbara's website to view all of her books
http://barbararaue.ca

© 2018 by Barbara Raue - All the photos in this book have been taken with my cameras. I own the rights to them.

www.ingramcontent.com/pod-product-compliance
Lightning Source LLC
Chambersburg PA
CBHW040231220526
45473CB00001B/206